**CENTRE FOR EDUCATIONAL RESEARCH
AND INNOVATION**

EDUCATION POLICY ANALYSIS

1998

ORGANISATION FOR ECONOMIC CO-OPERATION AND DEVELOPMENT

ORGANISATION FOR ECONOMIC CO-OPERATION AND DEVELOPMENT

Pursuant to Article 1 of the Convention signed in Paris on 14th December 1960, and which came into force on 30th September 1961, the Organisation for Economic Co-operation and Development (OECD) shall promote policies designed:

- to achieve the highest sustainable economic growth and employment and a rising standard of living in Member countries, while maintaining financial stability, and thus to contribute to the development of the world economy;
- to contribute to sound economic expansion in Member as well as non-member countries in the process of economic development; and
- to contribute to the expansion of world trade on a multilateral, non-discriminatory basis in accordance with international obligations.

The original Member countries of the OECD are Austria, Belgium, Canada, Denmark, France, Germany, Greece, Iceland, Ireland, Italy, Luxembourg, the Netherlands, Norway, Portugal, Spain, Sweden, Switzerland, Turkey, the United Kingdom and the United States. The following countries became Members subsequently through accession at the dates indicated hereafter: Japan (28th April 1964), Finland (28th January 1969), Australia (7th June 1971), New Zealand (29th May 1973), Mexico (18th May 1994), the Czech Republic (21st December 1995), Hungary (7th May 1996), Poland (22nd November 1996) and Korea (12th December 1996). The Commission of the European Communities takes part in the work of the OECD (Article 13 of the OECD Convention).

Publié en français sous le titre :

ANALYSE DES POLITIQUES D'ÉDUCATION
Édition 1998

TABLE OF CONTENTS

LIST OF TABLES, FIGURES AND BOXES

INTRODUCTION

National economies are restructuring themselves in ways that react to technological, social and economic change, and at best take advantage of them. A universal objective has been to give greater weight to the skills, knowledge and dispositions embodied in individuals. The value given to such human attributes, together with a continued rise in levels of education, income and wealth, drive increased demand for learning in its broadest sense. Education and training systems, institutions, schools and programmes are being asked to respond to higher expectations, and they must do so under very tight budgetary conditions and keen competition for public and private resources.

OECD Education Ministers have adopted lifelong learning for all, from infancy through adult years, as a concept giving coherence to the full range of such developments, expectations and constraints. At their 1997 meeting, OECD Labour Ministers endorsed the concept as an essential approach to ensuring that all, young people and adults, acquire and maintain the skills, abilities and dispositions needed to adapt to continuous changes in jobs and career paths. At their 1998 meeting, OECD Social Affairs Ministers endorsed the lifelong learning concept as an important means to reduce constraints on the way people spend time over the course of their life – in learning, in work, in leisure, in care-giving – and to promote a wider range of opportunities for people as they age.

The challenge is to make concrete the specific objectives of lifelong learning for all, and to identify those policy actions which will progressively turn the vision into reality. While public and official views on the aims of lifelong learning and its components vary among countries, there is everywhere an acknowledgment that much needs to be done. A gap remains between the rhetoric and the evaluation of policy actions and their impacts. To narrow that gap, this volume provides both an overarching framework which sets out key elements of a lifelong learning approach and an analysis of priority issues from a lifelong learning perspective. For the first time, a monitoring tool is advanced which can be used to take stock of the present state of play and to track progress toward the realisation of lifelong learning for all.

The framework for monitoring the implementation of lifelong learning is broad and comprehensive, spanning different stakeholders and providers and the responsibilities of different Ministries or administrations. It is intended to make more specific the links between aims, policies, practices and results, and to overcome the drift in the policy debate. Countries should be able to draw on findings of monitoring through this framework to address weaknesses and build on existing strengths in bringing about lifelong learning for all. Education systems that now commendably provide learning opportunities for nearly all young people into upper secondary education and, increasingly, beyond, will need, among other things, to introduce new forms of teaching and learning and new partnerships.

A lifelong learning approach calls for a sweeping shift in orientation, from institutions, schools and programmes to learners and learning. There is evidence of gaps in participation in learning at different ages over the lifespan, within and among countries. Development and learning opportunities in early childhood are uneven, as is participation in education by young adults around the years of upper secondary education. High estimated returns on public investment in education at this stage, relative to the costs, strengthen the case for renewed policy attention. Participation in education and training in adult years is directed at acquiring new skills and adapting existing ones rather than serving to compensate for lower levels of initial educational attainment, a finding which applies for countries as a whole and for women, among other groups, within countries. In addressing these gaps, policies will need to take into account consequences for all stages of lifelong learning. Increased rates of participation in education at younger ages do lead, and indeed should lead, to higher levels of participation at later stages of education and training. But, if adaptations are made to reinforce a learner-focus in programmes, teaching and learning which prepares young people and adults for continuous learning, higher rates of participation over the entire lifespan need not lead to proportional increases in costs. Interventions at early ages have been shown to reduce failure, repeating and drop-out in later stages, and individuals prepared and motivated to organise their own learning are also likely to be more efficient learners.

To motivate and prepare individuals for a lifetime of learning, educational programmes and teachers will need to be geared to individual needs. The teaching process and the organisation of learning opportunities will need to change. Thus, the policy focus needs to shift from who are the teachers to what such a change will mean for teaching. Teachers remain very much the heart of the matter, but policies will need to address learning conditions, resources and techniques as well as the expertise, preparation, professional development and incentives of those responsible for organising learning for young people. Even if the characteristics of the teaching force have not changed substantially over the past decade, it is clear that the role of the teacher continues to evolve sometimes in dramatic ways.

The focus on learning not only means that individual backgrounds, interests and choices need to be taken into account at any given stage, but also that learning is seen in the wider perspective of transitions and pathways through education and between education and employment. The transition from education into initial employment is now more varied, not least because of the choices young people themselves are making. While there is no single model, the most promising policy directions are those which situate programmes and options in a strong, stable framework that allows flexibility in learning pathways and provides preparation for the transition.

These pathways now frequently extend into tertiary education, where the dramatic growth of participation represents a strong response to demand, both individual and social. Public financing policies for tertiary education should also take into account the diversity of this demand, in the first instance by extending support to a much wider range of choices for what, when, how and where students now seek to learn. In this respect, tertiary education financing needs to embrace more fully a learner-centred, life-cyle orientation in which funds are paid through – and partly by – students. Under such a lifelong learning approach, all learners in tertiary education might be expected to contribute a share of the costs of their tuition and/or maintenance. However, students contributions towards tertiary education costs – whether achieved through tuition fees or deferred charges, loans for tuition fees or maintenance or graduate taxes – do not reduce the importance of a predominant public stake in financing tertiary education. The social returns to investment can be increased if public funding is both substantial and used strategically to balance recognition of the private gains from tertiary education with recognition of the possible adverse impact of large financial burdens incurred by students; to encourage efficiency on the part of providers and learners; and to promote flexibility, transparency and coherence as well as participation so that all who could benefit from tertiary-level studies enter the learning routes that best meet their needs. ■

Education Policy Analysis is now released at a different date than *Education at a Glance* – OECD *Indicators*. This reflects the continuing development of two distinctive, but highly complementary publications. While *Education Policy Analysis* draws on a wide range of information and findings generated in the OECD education work programme, it continues to make use of the OECD Education Database. Readers are referred to *Education at a Glance* 1997 for details on the definitions, methodologies and measures used.

LIFELONG LEARNING:
A monitoring framework and trends in participation

SUMMARY

Lifelong learning has been widely accepted as a goal by OECD countries. But there is a need to give this concept operational meaning – a way of translating it into concrete policy – and to develop a framework against which progress towards lifelong learning can be monitored.

This chapter identifies a number of ways in which lifelong learning can be operationalised, by placing new and distinctive requirements on education systems. It widens the scope of learning activity to which policy should be directed, to include study at every stage of life and in a wide variety of settings. Further, it places the individual at the centre of learning, by giving greater emphasis to demand and by aiming to build a capacity for self-directed learning. These principles have an important bearing on the structure of learning provision, on its content, on resource provision and on roles and responsibilities within the education system.

Member countries are converging in their interpretation of lifelong learning. Although strategies in various countries put different emphasis on various sectors of education, training and informal learning, countries share objectives spanning these sectors, such as diversify learning options supported by quality standards and robust qualification frameworks.

The chapter proposes a framework for monitoring progress towards lifelong learning. Indicators, it suggests, should address the scope and coverage of learning, the perspectives of different interests, the resources and inputs into education, learning processes, their outcomes and the context in which learning takes place. Present monitoring tools measure insufficiently the scope of activity and the range of outcomes. So such tools need to be improved.

In the meantime, however, there is already considerable hard evidence to indicate the degree to which people are participating in learning over the course of their lives. Participation in learning programmes is high through the early part of people's lives, but not in some countries in the early childhood or in the later teenage years, and patterns of participation in adult education and training differ more markedly among countries.

1. INTRODUCTION

In adopting the goal of "lifelong learning for all", OECD Education Ministers signalled a major departure from the narrower 1970s concept of recurrent education for adults (OECD, 1996). The new approach is a true "cradle to grave" view. It encompasses all purposeful learning activity undertaken with the aim of improving knowledge, skills and competence. It gives weight to building foundations for lifelong learning as well as to remedial second chances for adults. And it recognises that not only the settings of formal education but also the less formal settings of the home, the workplace, the community and society at large contribute to learning. Successful participation in lifelong learning may be said to display four characteristics: individuals are *motivated* to learn on a continuing basis; they are *equipped* with the necessary cognitive and other skills to engage in self-directed learning; they *have access to opportunities* for learning on a continuing basis; and they have the financial and cultural *incentives* to participate.

The very comprehensiveness of lifelong learning opens it up to multiple interpretations. Is the concept precise enough to be a useful guide for education and training policy? This chapter argues, first, that lifelong learning can be given operational meaning. Second, it provides evidence to suggest that Member countries are converging on an espousal of lifelong learning in its broader sense. Third, a proper assessment of progress on lifelong learning goals requires a more extensive set of indicators than is currently available, and the chapter outlines an organising framework for its development. Finally, even though available indicators are limited, an analysis of participation data shows that lifelong learning is a reality for a significant proportion of the OECD population. But much remains to be done to make it a reality for all. The present analysis makes a start in developing a framework in which progress towards this goal can be measured in the years ahead. Its aim is to inform the work both of the OECD and of others who seek to monitor the progress of lifelong learning, at both national and international levels.

2. LIFELONG LEARNING AS A POLICY GUIDE

Despite its all-embracing nature, the new concept of lifelong learning has several features that give it an operational significance for education and training policy in distinction from other approaches:

- the centrality of the learner and learner needs: that is, an orientation towards the "demand side" of education and training rather than just the supply of places;

- an emphasis on self-directed learning, and the associated requirement of "learning to learn" as an essential foundation for learning that continues throughout life;

- a recognition that learning takes place in many settings, both formal and informal; and

- a long-term view, that takes the whole course of an individual's life into consideration.

These features have important implications for some of the key parameters of education and training policy: for its *objectives*; for the *structure of provision*; for the *content, quality and relevance* of education and training; for *resource provision and management*, and for the *roles and responsibilities* of different partners and stakeholders.

Public and official views differ on the emphasis to be given to one or another of a wider range of *objectives* for education and training. A frequent bone of contention is whether education should pay more attention to meeting labour market needs or to preparing individuals for citizenship. Lifelong learning recognises the multiple missions of education and training – fostering an independent spirit of enquiry, personal development and fulfilment, preparation for working life and citizenship, enrichment of social and cultural life, and so on. The key here is the emphasis on developing within individuals the motivation and capacity to learn, which at different times can serve personal goals and those of employers, the community and society at large.

The concept also provides a framework in which diverse goals can be mutually reinforced. The need for a broad-based education seems to be increasingly emphasised by all with a stake in education – individuals, families, educationalists, enterprises, governments and society at large. This provides a way of harmonising what have been considered as competing objectives of education. A 1993 survey carried out in 12 OECD countries shows that the public at large expects schools to teach students qualities such as self-confidence, the skills and knowledge needed to get a job and the ability to live among people with different backgrounds (OECD, 1995). The public attaches to these general learning objectives greater importance than the learning of specific subjects. Within the working world, a range of generic skills – communication, linguistic abilities, creativity, team-work, problem-solving, familiarity with new technologies – are emerging as key attributes for obtaining employment and for adapting rapidly to changing work requirements. These skills need to be developed across school curricula, and are equally relevant for promoting a range of missions of education – good citizenship, individual fulfilment, an independent spirit of inquiry, awareness of social rights and responsibilities, as well as job readiness.

The recognition that learning takes place in diverse settings suggests a "systemic" view of the *structure of educational provision*, one which treats different forms of learning as part of a linked system. This raises several important questions for policies to address. Viewed over the lifetime, is the structure of provision, both formal and informal, matched properly to the structure of learning needs? Are there appropriate linkages and pathways between learning opportunities among the diverse settings and ways in which learning takes place? Are the resources, public and private, allocated to different sectors or providers appropriate in this perspective? The systemic approach puts a special responsibility on providers to recognise linkages to other sectors of provision and to what is happening in society more generally. No learning setting is an island.

With regard to the *content, quality and relevance* of education, the lifelong learning approach requires that a learning activity be evaluated in dynamic terms – it should not only contribute to new learning but, especially in early phases of an individual's life, also equip and motivate individuals for further learning, much of which will need to be self-directed. Individual motivation needs to be fuelled by the relevance of

the learning activity to one's needs and interests and preferred methods of learning. These factors emphasise the role of the learner in defining content and methods. One reason for high rates of early school leaving, for example, may lie in the poor match between the learning content and methods favoured by pupils and those chosen by the schools. Existing curricula are weak in building cross-curricular competencies and deficient in catering to students who are most suited to experiential learning. In the case of adults, studies have shown the importance of contextual learning and the need to tailor pedagogical approaches to suit older learners.

Existing approaches to *resources for education and training* are typically cast in sectoral terms. Resources devoted to the pathways and combinations of education and training actually undertaken by learners are not usually considered.[1] Nor are the resources devoted to informal learning. The lifelong learning approach offers a different optic – a systemic life-cycle approach that examines the resource requirements and the mobilisation of resources among providers and across sectors, both formal and informal. The costs and benefits of education and training, to the individual and to society, need to be evaluated in a way that is mindful of the timing of individual's engagement in different types and stages of learning over the lifespan, and of the links between them.

The wide range of activities that come under the rubric of lifelong learning makes it clear that the interests of a large range of stakeholders are involved. Strategies for lifelong learning highlight co-operation among different actors – operating at different educational levels and across sectoral boundaries which increasingly are blurring – and wider horizontal linkages between education policies and other domains of public policy. Such an approach requires that *roles and responsibilities* are shared. This is important both for mobilising resources for lifelong learning and for sharing the benefits that arise from it.

---

1. Chapter 3 in this volume provides an analysis of pathways through education and into work. Chapter 4 considers the resource implications of pathways followed through tertiary education.

These parameters illustrate the type of policy guidance that the concept of lifelong learning can provide. They also explain the popularity of the approach. The lifelong learning approach responds to the needs that have arisen as a result of the structural changes sweeping the OECD countries – changes spawned by forces including sustained periods of economic growth, technology, globalisation, deregulation of markets, demography, and the emergence of new economies. These pressures have significantly increased the importance of the "knowledge-based economy" as a determinant of social and economic advance. There is a convergence between the economic imperative, dictated by the needs of the knowledge society and of the labour market, and the societal need to promote social cohesion. Lifelong learning offers a credible response to these economic and social pressures.

The economic rationale for lifelong learning comes from two sources: from a need for continuous updating of skills – essential for structural adjustment, productivity growth, innovation and effective reallocation of human resources – and from change in the composition of skills demanded in the labour market. Employer requirements are less and less shaped by Taylorism, which focused on low-level repetitive skills. They increasingly demand a higher level of generic skills, of the type referred to above. Continuing learning, under these circumstances, is a productive investment, not simply a cost item – as important as physical capital, if not more – for the enterprise, the individual and the economy.

The distribution of learning opportunities is, however, quite uneven. There is well-documented evidence to show that initial education is a critical determinant of future training and learning, accentuating its effect on lifetime earnings. The education and training endowments of an individual serve as important determinants of the nature of employment, unemployment and earnings experience. Yet even though completion of secondary education is now close to universal in many countries, and participation in tertiary education a reality for half or more of a generation in some OECD countries, the social divides have not been satisfactorily breached through the educational and training process. Policies for social cohesion must therefore aim to ensure that conditions are in place to encourage and enable

everyone, young and mature, to participate and learn in education and training.

3. COUNTRY PERCEPTIONS

The broader concept of lifelong learning proposed by OECD Education Ministers is receiving wide support. It has been endorsed by their ministerial colleagues: Ministers of Labour (1997), Ministers of Social Affairs (1998), and by the Ministerial Council (1996, 1997). International organisations, such as UNESCO and the European Commission, have published reports espousing their ideas of the concept, at the same time as the OECD published its report *Lifelong Learning for All* (OECD, 1996). The European Union celebrated 1996 as the year of lifelong learning. New associations and non-governmental organisations have sprung up as have new academic journals dedicated to the concept and to the experience of strategies intended to foster its implementation.

Within individual countries, there is an emerging attempt to define and operationalise lifelong learning. Few countries have produced official national statements that set out comprehensive policies for lifelong learning but a number have issued green and white papers, commission reports and official statements pertaining to aspects of their education and training systems which can be considered part of a lifelong learning strategy. Some others are in the process of preparing official statements. Table 1.1 gives some illustrative examples. A number of patterns emerge from a review of these documents, and from the formulation of policy more generally with regard to lifelong learning.[2]

First, lifelong learning is increasingly conceptualised in the broader terms described in the preceding section. Few countries still use it to refer only to adult learning (Hungary is one exception); most have adopted the "cradle to grave" view. There is in particular increasing recognition of the twin importance of building foundation skills and providing opportunities later on, and of formal alongside informal opportunities. In Japan and in Scandinavia, the broader view of lifelong learning is already well established. Other countries are

2. The text which follows draws upon working papers developed as part of the OECD's activity on financing lifelong learning. Twelve countries have described policy strategies and provided detailed information.

Table 1.1 **Lifelong learning: definitions and objectives in key country documents**

AUSTRALIA

Document	Context	Main elements
Learning for Life: Review of Higher Education Financing and Policy (DEETYA, 1998).	While there is not yet a formal government policy on lifelong learning, this and other reviews and papers have created an active debate, revealing widespread support for the overall principle (Candy and Crebart, 1997).	Suggests that in its various forms (structured and unstructured), lifelong learning can provide individuals of all ages and backgrounds with skills and knowledge enhancing job chances and personal enrichment.

AUSTRIA

Document	Context	Main elements
Working and Coalition Agreements of governing parties (1990, 1994, 1996).	Education is a key part of the programme of Austrian governments, for economic and cultural reasons and to guard against extremism.	Working agreements since 1990 have used lifelong learning to refer to education and training of workers. Educational expansion is a priority in order to upgrade worker qualifications. The 1996 agreement established *Fachhochschule* (FHS) programmes to workers on unpaid leave. It also aimed to give adult education equal status with training, to make movement between tracks easier, to improve partnerships, to make apprenticeships less narrow, to expand counselling and to give schools more autonomy.
Advisory Council for Economic and Social Issues, (*Beschäftigungspolitik*) 1997.	This body incorporates the views of the social partners on educational matters.	A framework for lifelong learning in which initial training concentrates more on providing fundamental skills and knowledge on which later activities can build.

EUROPEAN UNION

Document	Context	Main elements
Learning and Training: Towards the Learning Society (European Union, 1995).	A framework document for the European Year of Lifelong Learning, 1996.	An important dimension is the role of education in constructing active European citizenship, recognising different cultural and economic approaches but also the commonality of European civilisation. Broad objectives also include acquisition of knowledge, new learning; school-business partnerships; fighting exclusion; language proficiency; equal treatment of human capital and other forms of investment.

FINLAND

Document	Context	Main elements
The Joy of Learning: a national strategy for lifelong learning, (Ministry of Education, 1997).	One of the few countries that has published a national statement outlining its vision of lifelong learning.	Promotion of broadly based and continuous learning, combining "learning careers" with activities in communities where people live and work. Policy objectives relate to personality, democratic values, social cohesion and internationalism as well as innovation, productivity, and competitiveness. Specific objectives include: strengthening learning foundations; providing a broad range of learning opportunities; recognising and rewarding learning regardless of where it takes place; building learning paths; improving teachers' and trainers' skills; and involving all relevant jurisdictions and players.

FRANCE

Document	Context	Main elements
Framework Law on Education (1989).	Established education as the top national priority.	Sets objective of educating 80% of youth population to upper secondary completion within 10 years, also addressing pre-school education. Five-year Law of 1993 adds right of young to vocational education.　......

ITALY

Document	Context	Main elements
Labour Agreement, 1996.	Lifelong Learning in Italy hitherto restricted to "right to education" of workers – 150 hours per year.	Recognises central role of human resources in production; envisions lifelong learning as fundamental incentive for competitiveness, supported by a balanced social model based on citizens' rights. Aims: to redefine the whole formative and learning system and the roles of institutions and individuals; to implement united national strategy administered by districts under national direction; to foster motivation to learn; to develop alternative tertiary institutions.

JAPAN

Document	Context	Main elements
Report on Lifelong Learning (Central Council for Education, 1981), *The First to Fourth and Final Reports on Educational Reform* (National Council on Educational Reform,1985-1987).	Japan was one of the first countries to express a comprehensive view of lifelong learning, for example in these documents.	Offered a concept of lifelong integrated education in which the entire education system would promote lifelong learning of individuals. The later document clarified that this meant free choice of individuals according to their own self-identified needs through life. Adult education based on hobbies and individual fulfilment is clearly delineated from occupational training. Lifelong learning aims to remedy problems arising from the pressures of a "diploma society", relating learning less to school achievement and providing spiritual enrichment and better use of leisure time.

KOREA

Document	Context	Main elements
Education Reform for New Education System (Presidential Commission on Educational Reform, 1996).	Recognised the need for a national framework of policies and infrastructure.	Learning opportunities should in particular promote access, support services, and arrangements for credit transfer, that open up study to people at times and places that meet their needs.

NETHERLANDS

Document	Context	Main elements
Lifelong Learning: the Dutch Initiative (Ministry of Education, Culture and Science, 1997).	An official government statement emerging from a year-long national Knowledge Debate, providing an Action Program to implement lifelong learning.	Recognises broadest meaning of lifelong learning, in which "initial education forms a major link". The rationale is both social and economic. Economically, people cannot be permitted to drop out of the labour market or hold marginal jobs. For social reasons, they should be given opportunities to prepare themselves adequately in various stages of their lives. The Action Program revolves around the employability of workers and job applicants; the employability of teachers; and the prevention of educational disadvantage through reorientation of education from the pre-school years.

NORWAY

Document	Context	Main elements
The New Competence (Ministry of Education, Research and Church Affairs, 1997).	Green paper on strategy for reforms of adult and continuing education, to be followed by legislative proposals.	The broader view of lifelong learning embracing youth and adulthood is well established. Priorities include initial education for young and for adults who need it, co-operation between government and social partners to meet workplace learning needs, and evaluation and recognition of learning wherever it takes place.

......

UNITED KINGDOM

Document	Context	Main elements
The Learning Age: a Renaissance for New Britain (Department for Education and Employment, 1998).	Green Paper setting out broad strategy of new administration, seeking consultation on a range of issues.	Advocates a regard for learning at all ages, from basic literacy to advanced scholarship, including formal and informal learning. Learning is seen as the key to prosperity and the foundation of success. Development of spiritual side of individuals and of citizenship considered important alongside economic objectives; the green paper stresses preparing citizens for active participation in all spheres. Government role seen as enabling citizens to take responsibility for themselves. Proposals include expanding further and higher education, creating "University for Industry", setting up individual learning accounts and promoting post-16 education, adult literacy, higher skill levels, and better teaching and learning standards.

UNITED STATES

Document	Context	Main elements
President Clinton's Ten-point plan for education (Delci, 1997).	The closest to a national mission statement in a country with multiple formulations of objectives which have mentioned lifelong learning for at least 20 years (e.g. College Board, 1978).	Includes spirit of lifelong learning in many respects. Programme includes strengthening of teaching, independent reading by students by 3rd grade, parental involvement in early learning, making two years of post-secondary education the norm, improving adult education and skills, and connecting every school and library to the Internet by 2000.

beginning to recognise the need to restructure the school system to meet the requirements of a new economy and to prepare individuals for complex social roles. The Czech Republic presents an example of this approach.

Second, there is a shared view across countries of the main reasons for lifelong learning. Most recognise that there is both an economic and a social imperative, and a number of countries as well as the European Union put a stress on citizenship. Countries that have most explicitly tried to formulate a comprehensive strategy, such as Finland, the Netherlands and the United Kingdom, have taken care to stress a balanced approach. However, there are differences in the emphasis placed on the economic and the social: Japan puts particular stress on spiritual development and a better enjoyment of life, while countries such as Austria, Australia and Canada, emphasise skill training for improving employability and competitiveness, at the same time as recognising the importance of learning to personal development and citizenship.

Third, within the broader umbrella of lifelong learning, countries are operationalising the concept in different ways and differ in the emphasis placed on various aspects or sectors of lifelong learning as there are country differences in the urgency of perceived needs. Some countries have made specific commitments to apply the goals of lifelong learning to the strengthening of teaching and learning at the school level. Others are putting the accent on improving post-secondary and adult training opportunities.

Fourth, despite this diversity there are, across countries, a number of common elements on which lifelong strategies are being based. These include: a diversification of learning options, accompanied by a search for a quality guarantee; extension of the certification and recognition system, including easier credit transfer; greater emphasis on the responsibility of individual actors and stakeholders, with governments responsible for providing a common framework; decentralisation of the delivery of services; and partnerships that draw on the interests and resources of all stakeholders.

Finally, the logic of lifelong learning strategies, and the arguments supporting them, are often phrased in calls for creating a "culture" of learning, an ethic of learning and an environment that is supportive of learning in all its forms. With the demand for such society-wide changes, which is a long-term project that must involve the participation of all stakeholders and citizens, a contradictory trend can also be observed. On the one hand there is a limited recognition that a commitment to lifelong learning involves major, not simply incremental, changes. On the other hand, there is also some evidence of a resistance to change.

4. **ELEMENTS OF A MONITORING FRAMEWORK**

In agreeing to implement strategies for lifelong learning, OECD Education Ministers invited the Organisation to "monitor progress" towards the realisation of this goal (OECD, 1996). Given the sheer scope, volume, and variety of lifelong learning, this is a complex task that includes at least three elements: an evaluation of whether policies point in appropriate directions; an assessment of the impact of the policies and programmes; and the development of indicators that assess whether various targets are being met. Policy reviews and impact studies of lifelong learning require a much more extensive data and indicators set.

A framework is needed to determine which of the existing indicators remain useful, which need to be re-interpreted in the lifelong learning perspective and what new indicators must be developed. This framework will, in particular, need to consider the following areas of lifelong learning: its *scope or coverage*; the variety of *perspectives*; types of resources or *inputs*; nature of learning *outcomes*; nature of *processes* that mediate between various actors, and between inputs and outcomes; and the *context* in which learning takes place.

The *scope or coverage* of available indicators needs to be broadened to cover all purposeful learning in various phases of the life-cycle. Full coverage needs to be given to the "lifelong" aspect: existing data are particularly deficient with respect to learning in early childhood and among older adults. Another element is sometimes described as the "life-wide" aspect: it concerns the variety of both formal and informal learning that takes place in each life-phase. The new emphasis on informal learning highlights the need for data on experiences outside educational institutions, which are particularly lacking. By their nature, these experiences are harder to record and quantify, but there is nevertheless scope to develop improved assessments of such activity.

A *range of perspectives*: Lifelong learning involves a wide range of stakeholders, each with different types of information needs for decision-making.

Individual learning outcomes remain at the centre but the whole structure of provision needs to be taken into account from the perspectives of individuals, providers, governments (at different levels), employers, families and society at large. The information needs of different stakeholders differ from each other. Governments require for example information on behaviour patterns of other stakeholders – not least the learners – who both provide input to and impinge on the outcomes of learning activity, in order to consider the full consequences of policy decisions. They also need different types of information for making various decisions with different time horizons: some policies and programmes can be applied in the short and medium-term but often results can only be evaluated over the long-term. Other stakeholders like employers and providers have different information needs. Information for individual learners on the array of learning opportunities, their forms, costs and intended or likely outcomes, is uneven and not easily accessed; this is seen as a crucial element in a lifelong learning approach which relies on informed choices of learners and their families and envisages the match between backgrounds and interests and the types and forms of learning options as a key to successful learning.

Existing indicators on *inputs* – human, financial and technological, including methods of teaching and learning – are probably strongest, but new information is needed on informal learning as this area increases in importance. More information is required on the effectiveness of different approaches to teaching and learning. The rapidly changing technology of learning may alter the cost, availability, and effectiveness of different modes of teaching and learning. The role of teachers, and of the learning environment, may also be significantly changed. These aspects, as discussed in Chapter 2, need to be captured in any monitoring of the realisation of lifelong learning.

Information gaps are arguably most pressing in the area of *outcomes*. Some outcome measures, such as educational attainment, are well known and widely available, but there is a great dearth of information on assessment of skills and competence acquired as an outcome of the learning process. This is especially the case with informal learning. Measures to identify, certify and recognise such learning are needed. A broader definition of outcomes includes attitudinal and motivational behaviour. While critical for lifelong learning, information in this area is especially deficient.

A monitoring effort needs to develop information on *processes*, revealing the links and interfaces between levels and among providers and sectors. Information on transition processes and pathways between initial learning, work and further learning are key. So, too, is information on complementarity and articulation of programmes and learning opportunities, and on co-operation between the various stakeholders involved in teaching and learning. Indicators need to be developed on such issues as the flexibility of choice among different pathways, barriers to and incentives for learning, and the impact of the processes on motivation and attitudes, where information is sparse.

Finally, the nature and quality of learning is profoundly influenced by the learning *context*. Given the importance that the lifelong learning approach places on the systemic view, information is needed on how different types of provision are linked together and cater to the needs of people in their different life phases. Information is needed on the attributes of a "culture" of learning, attitudinal changes that contribute to such a culture, and how they can be given institutional expression.

5. PARTICIPATION IN LIFELONG LEARNING

A monitoring framework that captures all of these areas of lifelong learning would be complex. Work continues in the OECD's INES programme to examine the conceptual and empirical bases for developing a more comprehensive set of indicators which can be used to assess progress towards the realisation of lifelong learning for all. Recently-developed indicators shed light on one important aspect of lifelong learning, namely participation in learning activities. The available data do not cover all age groups, do not touch on quality aspects and are not available for all Member countries. Nonetheless, they reveal several

patterns and trends from the perspective of participation in learning activities over the life-span.

First, lifelong participation in learning is already a reality for a significant minority of the OECD population. This can be observed from Figure 1.1, which brings together enrolment information in formal education (the solid line) and participation in adult education and training (broken line), for the nine OECD countries for which both sets of information are available. These data combine two very different concepts and coverage, one based largely on full-time education, and the other on largely part-time participation (see Box 1.1). Virtually universal education up to age 15 is well-known, testifying to the rapid progress of OECD countries over the last three decades. What is less well-known is the frequency of participation in adult years: measured over the preceding twelve month period, more than 10 per cent of the age-cohort is engaged in some form of education and training even at age 60-65 (OECD and Statistics Canada, 1997).

Second, the heavily front-loaded pattern of participation is evident. After age 3, participation in formal education increases sharply, reaching close to universal coverage in primary and lower secondary years. Participation begins to decrease around age 15, relatively moderately at first and sharply after 18. The decline continues at age 20-21 but by this age a substantial number are participating in adult education and training. By the age initial formal education commonly is completed, over two-thirds of adults (aged 25-34) in the average OECD country have gained upper-secondary qualifications, and about one-quarter have completed tertiary education (OECD, 1997a, Indicator A2).

Third, participation in organised education and training continues to fall during adulthood. The proportion of respondents who reported having participated during the 12 months before being questioned in the International Adult Literacy Survey (OECD and Statistics Canada, 1997) peaks at age 21 (at almost 50 per cent) and declines gradually. The decline is particularly noticeable after age 40, with an even sharper decline after age 50.

Figure 1.1
Participation in education and training over the life-span
Percentage of age cohort enrolled in formal education (age 3 to 29), and participation in adult education and training (age 16 to 65), unweighted mean, for nine countries*, 1994-1995

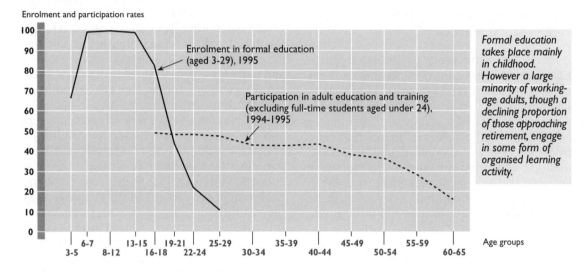

Enrolment and participation rates

Enrolment in formal education (aged 3-29), 1995

Participation in adult education and training (excluding full-time students aged under 24), 1994-1995

Formal education takes place mainly in childhood. However a large minority of working-age adults, though a declining proportion of those approaching retirement, engage in some form of organised learning activity.

Age groups

* Belgium, Canada, Ireland, Netherlands, New Zealand, Sweden, Switzerland (French and German for IALS), United Kingdom, United States.
Sources: OECD Education Database and International Adult Literacy Survey.
Data for Figure 1.1: *page 74.*

BOX 1.1 COMPARING YOUTH AND ADULT PARTICIPATION RATES

Figure 1.1 summarises participation trends over the lifespan by combining data on the proportion of young people in formal education with estimates of the proportion of adults who undergo some type of education or training in a given year. This serves to illustrate the pattern of learning over the lifecycle. However, the juxtaposition of the two data sets should be interpreted with caution, for two reasons.

First, they relate to different types of learning. The youth series is drawn from national records of students enrolled in educational institutions, mainly full-time. The adult series is based on a question in the International Adult Literacy Survey (IALS) about whether the respondent has participated in *any* organised learning activity for *any* length of time during the previous twelve months. The question includes for example workshops, on-the-job-training and recreational courses.

Second, some clarification is needed about data coverage in the age-range in which the two data series overlap. In order to avoid counting young adults still in initial education as undertaking "adult education", all full-time students aged 16-24 are left out of the calculation of adult participation rates in IALS. So for this age-group, the broken line represents mainly a different group of people from the solid line, showing them as a proportion of all *non-students* (so the two participation rates cannot be added together). For everyone aged 25 and over, the broken line shows the total of all people studying, including those who remain in or have returned to formal education. Thus the solid line, which looks at students in formal education up to the age of 29, effectively represents a subset of the broken line for the final 4 years shown.

Figure 1.2
Gender and lifelong learning

A. Educational attainment of women compared to men, 25 to 34 and 55 to 64 year-olds, 1995
Percentage difference in average years of completed education

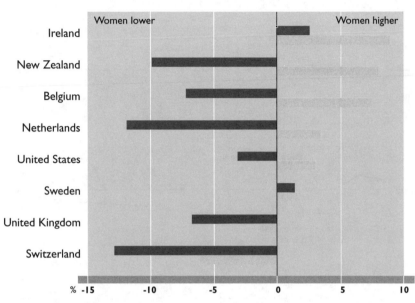

Source: OECD Education Database.

B. Participation in adult education and training of women compared to men, 25 to 34 and 55 to 64 year-olds, 1994-1995
Percentage difference in participation rates

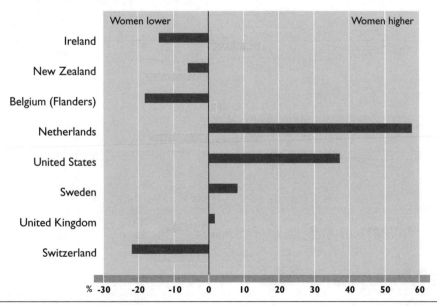

Women of about 30 are on average as well educated as men, but participate less in adult education and training; those of about 60 have received less initial education, but are engaged in as much current learning as their male contemporaries.

Source: International Adult Literacy Survey.
Data for Figures 1.2A and 1.2B: pages 74-75.

Figure 1.3 **Participation over the life-span: country variations**

——— Enrolment in formal education (aged 3-29), 1995

- - - - - Participation in adult education and training (excluding full-time students aged under 24), 1994-1995

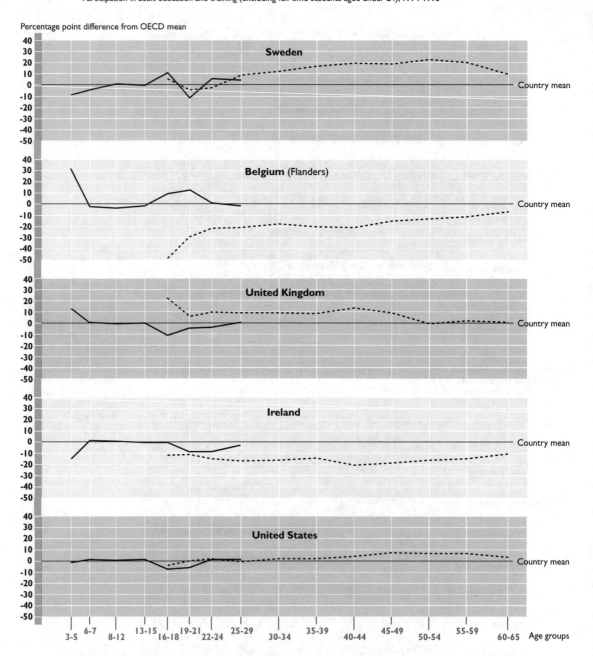

Percentage point difference from OECD mean

Countries with high youth participation in formal education do not always have high participation in adult education and training.

Sources: OECD Education Database and International Adult Literacy Survey.

Data for Figure 1.3: page 74.

As a proxy for participation in all learning activity, the information in Figure 1.1 is clearly an underestimate. The broken line would lie further up, indicating higher rates of participation, if account could be taken of the unorganised and informal learning experience that takes place in a variety of settings, on which, unfortunately, internationally comparable data are currently not available. As informal learning increases in importance, through the wider use of the Internet for example, the hidden level of participation can be expected to rise further. Detailed information on the quality of training is not available, but its duration can be used as one proxy. A large proportion of the training obtained is for a very limited period. In four of nine countries for which comparable data are available, less than 30 per cent of workers receiving training spent two weeks or more doing so.[3] What Figure 1.1 also shows is that, for most post-school age groups, more than two-thirds of the population do not participate in organised learning activities each year.

Fourth, the high participation in initial education, shown in Figure 1.1, should eventually drive a rising rate of participation in adult education. Consider the following two indicators. First, on present graduation trends the proportion of 25-64 year olds with upper secondary education will rise from 60 per cent to 73 per cent (unweighted country average) between 1995 and 2015 (OECD, 1997b). Second, people with superior education levels are far more likely to participate in adult education and training: adults with upper-secondary education (but not tertiary) were between 32 per cent and 38 per cent more likely to participate than those with only lower-secondary, in every country surveyed except Sweden where participation is high for all educational groups (OECD and Statistics Canada, 1997). So as today's young, better educated cohorts grow older, adult learning rates are likely to rise substantially, even if the form, frequency and duration of learning activities in adulthood may be expected to evolve. Moreover the rising trend in participation in full-time education will, in itself, increasingly extend the solid line in Figure 1.1 to the right as an increasing proportion of mature adults are coming back to both secondary and tertiary level education.

Fifth, even though women are now about equally represented, on average, at all stages of formal education, there are significant differences in participation and attainment across the life cycle. Examples of two significant types of difference are shown in Figure 1.2. This graph looks at the differences between the sexes among adults of particular ages, both in terms of levels of initial education and in terms of whether they have participated in organised learning over the previous twelve months. Greater equality in initial education in the past 20 years has meant that in a majority of countries, women aged 25 to 34 have completed more years of initial education than men of the same age. But men are more likely at this age to be currently engaged in learning; they receive for example a disproportionate share of training at work. For an older cohort, aged 55-64, women in the majority of the countries have completed fewer years of initial education than men. But interestingly, in half of the countries, they do not in this age-range participate on average less than men, probably because work-related learning has by this age become relatively less important.

Sixth, there are marked differences among OECD countries. Figure 1.3 shows examples of how youth and adult participation rates in individual countries compare to the average for nine OECD countries. First, in Sweden, it can be seen that participation is high at almost every age beyond early childhood – including young people in upper-secondary education aged 16-18, those continuing in formal education in their mid-20s and adults participating at all ages. Second, in Belgium (Flanders) there is a high staying-on rate for young people, but a low rate of participation in adult education and training. Conversely, in the United Kingdom staying-on rates are low but adult participation is high.

---

3. Detailed country data are provided in the statistical annex, Table 1.A, page 76. Over time, it is not evident that training of short duration leads to less learning. Improvements in the foundations provided in compulsory schooling through the first years of tertiary education could equip individuals to be more efficient learners, enabling the realisation of learning objectives in a shorter period of time.

In Ireland participation in both respects is below average outside the compulsory years. Finally, the United States is about average on both counts. High youth participation and high adult participation do not tend to go together. Canada, New Zealand and Switzerland are similar to the United Kingdom in combining low youth with high adult rates.[4] So the Swedish and Irish cases seem to be the exception. For some countries, there appears to be a compensatory difference between enrolment in formal education in the early phases of life and participation in adult learning activities later on.

Looking more closely at country differences in participation in education, the most important differences come just before and just after compulsory schooling. At age 3, for example, six of the 25 countries reported enrolment rates in pre-school education of less than 20 per cent, at the same time as six others reported rates over 60 per cent, with virtually universal participation in France and Belgium (Figure 1.4). Differences at age 4 are not as sharp but still very large. Country differences again manifest themselves as full-time upper secondary education ends. For the age group 14-17, in seven of the 26 countries participation rates were reported to be below 90 per cent. Turkey and Mexico ranked the lowest with rates less than 50 per cent. By age 18-19, nine of the 25 countries have enrolment rates (upper secondary and tertiary combined) below 50 per cent (Figure 1.5).

Figure 1.4   Pre-school participation, 1995

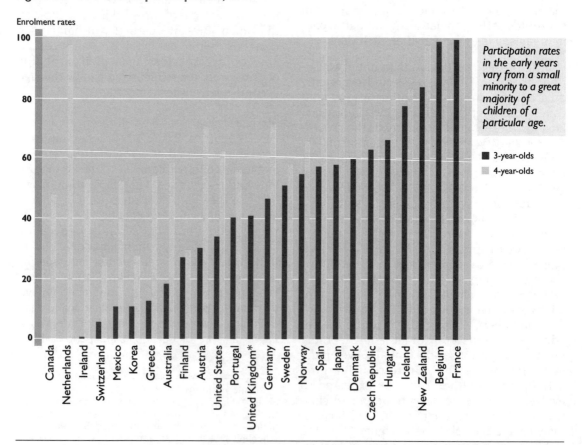

Enrolment rates

Participation rates in the early years vary from a small minority to a great majority of children of a particular age.

■ 3-year-olds
▨ 4-year-olds

* Over 80 per cent of 4-year-olds in the United Kingdom are already enrolled, beyond pre-school, in primary education.
Source: OECD Education Database.
Data for Figure 1.4: page 75.

Figure 1.5   Teenage participation, 1995

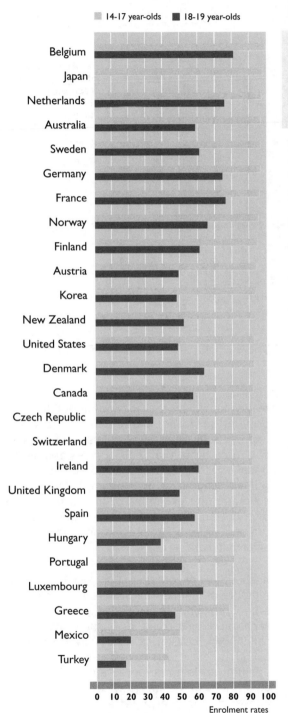

14-17 year-olds   18-19 year-olds

Belgium
Japan
Netherlands
Australia
Sweden
Germany
France
Norway
Finland
Austria
Korea
New Zealand
United States
Denmark
Canada
Czech Republic
Switzerland
Ireland
United Kingdom
Spain
Hungary
Portugal
Luxembourg
Greece
Mexico
Turkey

0 10 20 30 40 50 60 70 80 90 100
Enrolment rates

Source: OECD Education Database.
Data for Figure 1.5: page 75.

After age 19, there is a steady decrease in participation in education, as shown in Figure 1.1. By age 22, nine of the 22 countries report participation rates above 30 per cent while three have rates below 15 per cent.[5]

In some countries participation drops rapidly after compulsory schooling; in others, a majority remain enrolled throughout their teens.

Seventh, there has been some reduction in inter-country differences over the past decade. Enrolment in secondary schools increased virtually everywhere, with large increases especially in those countries where participation rates were comparatively modest in 1985 (Figure 1.6). Increases have been most marked in Portugal, Spain, New Zealand and the United Kingdom.

This observation is further supported by the information on country trends in participation in tertiary education. The proportion of the age group going on to some form of tertiary education has increased over the ten year period, in some cases substantially (OECD, 1997*b* and 1998). Country differences, while still large in 1995, are less than they were in 1985. The increase has been particularly notable in a few countries: Canada, Norway, Spain and Sweden. Enrolments in tertiary-level institutions have expanded in some cases to 40 per cent of the age group leaving secondary schools. The expansion of participation in tertiary education is one of the major educational and social developments of the past twenty-five years. Further increases in participation rates seem likely, both in countries that have led as well as those that have lagged behind this trend.

Finally, there are large within-country differences in participation. These can be best illustrated with reference to the data on adult education and training, which are particularly unevenly distributed.[6] A high proportion of opportunities are

4. Data for nine countries are presented in the statistical annex, page 74.

5. See OECD (1997*a* and 1997*b*). Complete country data of enrolment in formal education by single year of age are provided in the statistical annex, Table 1.B, page 76.

6. Detailed country data are provided in the statistical annex, Table 1.A, page 76.

Figure 1.6
Towards universal participation of youth, 1985 and 1995
Percentage of 14 to 17 year-olds enrolled in education

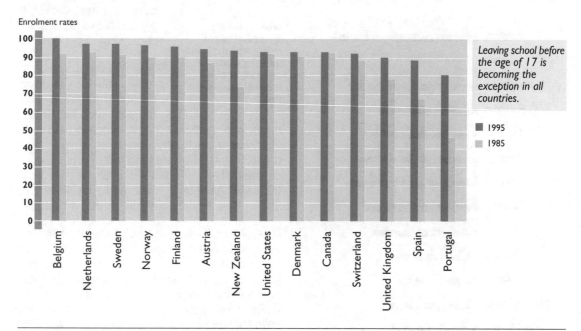

Leaving school before the age of 17 is becoming the exception in all countries.

■ 1995
□ 1985

Source: OECD Education Database.
Data for Figure 1.6: page 75.

organised through employers, so unemployed individuals, those who work in small enterprises or those who enter the labour market with low qualifications have less access to adult education and training opportunities. These patterns indicate where policy should be focused if the gaps are to be filled.

Identifying the gaps

The data on participation can help identify where more attention needs to be given to the provision of organised learning opportunities, even though this is only one part of the lifelong learning framework. They do not show the quality of learning experiences, the incidence of informal learning or the degree to which various opportunities link together into a coherent framework for learning that builds over the life span.

The data show that lifelong learning is already a reality for a segment of the OECD population, but there is clearly much to be done to make it a

reality "for all": more than two-thirds of the adult population do not participate in organised learning activities each year. In some European countries more than half of the working-age population has received little education beyond primary schooling. There are important gaps in coverage and examples of inequities in the distribution of education and training opportunities, in both formal education programmes and adult learning.

In about half of countries supplying data, only a minority of children participate in formal pre-school programmes before the age of 4. But the variation among countries is substantial: early childhood education is virtually universal in a few countries, but others have a long way to go in opening up learning opportunities for young children. While there is clearly an emerging consensus on the importance of providing stimulating environments for very young children, there is considerable debate across OECD countries on whether enrolment in organised and formal provision outside the family is necessarily the best approach for the very young. A key question concerns the quality of provision on which, unfortunately, data are lacking. Policy choices must take into account the competition for public and private resources and how the relationships between families and schools are affected by an expansion of pre-primary education.

Several countries now retain nearly all young people in secondary school until age 17, but there is less than full retention in upper secondary education. Early school leaving and high failure rates are important problems, as those without full secondary education confront more limited and poor labour market prospects.[7] Weak school performance has been shown to be associated with low socio-economic status, so the problems are both more concentrated and difficult. Reforms of school curricula to foster greater motivation for learning and a better integration of vocational and general studies and work-related experience seem to be particularly promising approaches to bring these learners up to a minimum level of education but also to equip them for continued learning in later life.

Continued growth in participation in tertiary education raises new challenges, opportunities and dilemmas for policy. These include how to provide a range of tertiary-level learning opportunities to a more diverse population of learners at this level; how to define and maintain quality across the range of study programmes and options; how to ensure coherence and transparency while meeting diverse learning needs and interests; how to mobilise resources and improve efficiency in the light of high volume participation; how to respond to the needs of those who do *not* participate in tertiary education.[8] It is now being recognised that the boundaries between establishments and programmes among and within levels should be seen as flexible and to some extent overlapping. The distinction between vocational, professional and general education at secondary and tertiary levels is one of degree and emphasis. The bypassing of sectoral boundaries in an effort to reinforce the continuity of learning is emphasised in a lifelong approach.[9]

6. **CONCLUSIONS**

The concept of lifelong learning has been significantly broadened since the 1970s. As an all-embracing and comprehensive concept it can mean very different things to different people. This chapter illustrates the ways in which the broader concept can be useful for guiding education and training policy, and provides evidence to suggest that OECD countries are adopting it. The chapter has also shown how the lifelong learning approach can be useful for identifying the indicators needed for monitoring progress on both the policy objectives and more narrowly defined targets.

A framework that monitors progress towards lifelong learning in a comprehensive way will be a complex system. It will need to take account of different perspectives – of individuals, of providers and of societies. Old indicators have to be re-interpreted and new ones need to be developed. Too little is still known about early childhood education, motivation to learn, informal learning and learning in older age. Information remains deficient on what is the most effective pedagogy for different groups of learners. In examining the structure of provision, information on pathways, standards and certification has high priority.

Monitoring progress will be a difficult and always imperfect exercise: it will never be possible to construct fully adequate indicators of all the informal learning that occurs in people's lives. But it will nevertheless be possible to build on our present understanding as an aid to policy development. Already it is possible to show that only a minority of the OECD population is participating in education and training on a lifelong basis. There is a considerable distance to go in making learning a reality "for all", even without considerations of content, quality, and relevance. Attaining the goal would be costly but it is also an investment. It is a realisable ambition, if it is pursued as a long-term effort to which all partners contribute. ∎

---

7. On transition, see Chapter 3 of this volume.

8. See OECD (1997*b* and 1998) and Chapter 4 of this volume.

9. On patterns of participation in the first years of tertiary education, see OECD (1997*b*) and OECD (1998).

References

BEIRAT FÜR WIRTSCHAFTS – UND SOCIALFRAGEN (1997), *Beschäftigungspolitik*, Wien, Austria.

CANDY, P. and **CREBART, R.** (1997), "Australia's progress towards lifelong learning", in *Comparative Studies on Lifelong Learning Policies*, NIER and UIE, Tokyo, Japan.

CENTRAL COUNCIL FOR EDUCATION (1981), *On Lifelong Integrated Education*, Tokyo, Japan.

COLLEGE BOARD (1978), *Lifelong Learning during Adulthood, An Agenda for Research: Future Directions for a Learning Society*, College Entrance Examination Board, New York, United States.

DELCI, M. (1997), "Lifelong learning in the United States", in *Learning to Monitor Lifelong Learning*, Working Paper prepared for the OECD, NCRVE, University of California, Berkeley, United States.

DEPARTMENT FOR EDUCATION AND EMPLOYMENT (1998), *The Learning Age: A Renaissance for a New Britain*, Green Paper submitted to the Parliament, February, London, United Kingdom.

DEPARTMENT FOR EMPLOYMENT, EDUCATION, TRAINING AND YOUTH AFFAIRS (1998), *Learning for Life: Review of Higher Education Financing and Policy*, Social Report, Canberra, Australia.

EUROPEAN UNION (1995), *Learning and Training: Towards the Learning Society*, White Paper, November, Brussels, Belgium.

GENDRON, B. (1997), "Lifelong learning in France", in *Learning to Monitor Lifelong Learning*, Working Paper prepared for the OECD, NCRVE, University of California, Berkeley, United States.

MINISTRY OF EDUCATION (1997), *The Joy of Learning: A National Strategy for Lifelong Learning*, Committee Report, No. 14, Helsinki, Finland.

MINISTRY OF EDUCATION, CULTURE AND SCIENCE (1998), *Lifelong Learning: The Dutch Initiative*, Den Haag, The Netherlands.

MINISTRY OF EDUCATION, RESEARCH AND CHURCH AFFAIRS (1997), *The New Competence: The Basis for a Total Policy for Continuing Education and Training for Adults*, (Abridged version translated from Norwegian), Committee Proposals submitted to the Ministry, Oslo, Norway.

NATIONAL COUNCIL ON EDUCATIONAL REFORM (1987), *Fourth and Final Report on Educational Reform*, Tokyo, Japan.

PRESIDENTIAL COMMISSION ON EDUCATIONAL REFORM (1996), *Education Reform for a New Education System: To Meet the Challenges of Information and Globalisation Era*, Seoul, Republic of Korea.

OECD (1995), *Public Expectations in the Final Stage of Compulsory Education*, Paris.

OECD (1996), *Lifelong Learning for All*, Paris.

OECD (1997a), *Education at a Glance – OECD Indicators 1997*, Paris.

OECD (1997b), *Education Policy Analysis 1997*, Paris.

OECD (1998), *Redefining Tertiary Education*, Paris.

OECD AND STATISTICS CANADA (1997), *Literacy Skills for the Knowledge Society – Further Results of the International Adult Literacy Survey*, Paris.

CHAPTER 2

TEACHERS FOR TOMORROW'S SCHOOLS

SUMMARY

Schools are being asked to play a key role in helping OECD societies adapt to social and economic change; they will not be able to meet such challenges unless teachers are at the centre of the process. This chapter argues that attempts to transform teaching and learning must not neglect the teachers themselves, whose expertise, motivation and organisation needs to be brought to bear in support of change, rather than being neglected or, worse still, regarded as an obstacle.

The transformation of teaching is no easy task, given the size and diversity of the teaching force. Few generalisations can be made across all countries. School teachers compose from 2 to 4 per cent of OECD workforces. The majority are women, at the primary level, in most countries, but this varies across countries, and in secondary schools there are many men – who for example compose three-quarters of upper secondary German and Japanese teachers. Lower secondary teacher salaries vary from 0.8 time average national income per head to 2.9 times. A high proportion of teachers are in their 50s – this too varies widely, from 40 per cent in Sweden to 13 per cent in Austria.

Both younger and older teachers need to be involved in a renewal of skills and attitudes to create schools appropriate for the challenges ahead. Increasingly, professional development is being interpreted to mean more than upgrading the skills of individual teachers, with great stress put on learning that creates lasting improvements in the practices of schools. There are signs that there is still far too little investment in such development, although by its nature it can be hard to measure.

Professional development must be seen in conjunction with fundamental changes in the organisation and methods of schools. Some schools and classes have been transformed by practices such as team teaching, the imaginative use of technology and opening up teaching and learning more to families, communities, public organisations and private entities. There is not yet clear evidence that these are general practices, and indeed they remain patchy. Far from such developments representing alternatives that diminish the role of the teacher, they demand still greater professional skills.

Without change, there is a danger that technological and other developments will make schools and teachers seem increasingly irrelevant, especially to young people. Teacher professionalism should not obstruct change but be redefined to become part of it. The professionalism of the 21st century must include expertise, openness, use of technology and the capacity to adapt and collaborate continuously within schools and networks that are learning organisations.

1. INTRODUCTION

Schools are being charged with a growing range of responsibilities. Their role is seen as central in helping societies adapt to profound social, economic and cultural changes. Their capacity to fulfill these expectations, however, depends crucially on their own ability to manage change, and in particular on whether teachers are able to develop positive and effective strategies to meet the needs of tomorrow's schools.

This chapter considers the role of teachers in the transformation of schools, drawing on a range of recent OECD research and data on teachers today.[1] It starts, in Section 2, by emphasising the need to put teachers at the centre of strategies for lifelong learning, which will require major endeavours among large and diverse teaching forces. Section 3 looks at the characteristics of today's teachers, showing that even though the picture of an aged profession is an undue simplification, there is clearly a need for renewal of teacher knowledge and skills. As Section 4 sets out, professional development is most successful when it goes beyond the updating of knowledge, and aims to be the motor of educational innovation. Teacher involvement is a necessary, but not a sufficient condition for successful reform. Schools as organisations, and school systems, need to decide whether they are willing to consider radical changes to traditional structures. Section 5 explores the degree to which education systems are accepting a range of practices that depart from single teachers in classrooms, adopting conventional teaching methods. Fundamental change should not undermine teacher professionalism, but rather transform it. Section 6 concludes by discussing the role of the professional teacher in the changed environment of 21st century schools.

2. REFORM AND LIFELONG LEARNING – BRINGING TEACHERS BACK INTO THE PICTURE

A plethora of recent educational reforms across OECD countries (see eg. OECD, 1996a; Eurydice, 1996) has aimed to improve educational outcomes for young people. Central to the desired outcomes has been the objective, in theory at least, of making school education the foundation of lifelong learning. Schools are expected to develop an initial set of skills, motivation and culture that will serve on a lifetime basis – for all and not just the well-educated. This marks a significant change from a model that saw school education as a more self-contained process, and challenges education systems to consider more directly their impact on mature citizens' ability to continue learning and to adapt to life's challenges. But while the lifelong learning model may be accepted in principle, it is less clear in practice whether new expectations and aims have created a shared understanding of what it means for initial schooling to build the foundation of skills, motivation and culture that will serve all over their lifetimes.

How far schools are able to transform to become oriented towards lifelong learning will hinge to a large extent on the contribution of teachers. The quality of learning depends directly on the teacher in the classroom, and indirectly on the key part that teachers play in the organisation of schools and school systems. New curricula or assessment policies, or investment in new information and communication technologies, will only produce significant change if they are understood and applied by teachers.

One danger with debate on school improvement and reform is that the focus on what should occur in schools – such as high quality teaching and learning – can neglect the human beings who must make these things happen. A focus on "learning" is necessary, especially in emphasising outcomes of education for students, but risks playing down the importance of the teacher by regarding him or her as just one of many influences. Even a focus on "teaching" can overlook the importance of the expertise, motivation and organisation of the staff who carry it out. The delivery of good teaching by a particular corps of professionals needs to be recognised as central to learning outcomes.

---

1. The chapter has been developed as part of the CERI project on "Schooling for Tomorrow". It remains the case, as emphasised in the 1990 OECD study *The Teacher Today*, that teachers in other settings, especially vocational education and training, but also higher and adult education, tend to be much neglected (compared with such matters as curricula, accreditation, student support, etc.).

This centrality of teachers is not always properly recognised, especially at the political level when the case is made for reform. A worldwide review of reform proposals (Villegas-Reimars and Reimers, 1996; see also UNESCO, 1998) describes the teacher as the "missing voice in educational reform":

> "...[in] calls for reform and in the options which are brought forth to change schools, there is surprisingly little attention to the role of teachers. Some of the proposals for change advocate 'teacher-proof' innovations, which can sustain the impetus for change in spite of the teachers. In some other cases, teachers are absent from the discourse about change. In yet other cases, the role of teachers is not central to the proposals for change." (p. 469)

In recognising the importance of teachers in implementing reform, it is not enough to regard teacher policy as a personnel issue. While pay, work conditions and qualifications matter acutely to teachers and influence quality by making the profession more or less attractive, teachers cannot be regarded as mere foot-soldiers implementing orders from above. They are at the heart of the process. Successful reform does not take place "despite" teachers, but rather ensures that their contribution is maximised.

3. MANY TEACHERS, DIVERSE PROFILES

Efforts to involve teachers in educational change need to be directed at an extremely large and by no means homogeneous group of people. The characteristics of teachers have to be taken into account when developing policies affecting in-service training, professional development and the conditions in which teachers operate, all of which can help equip schools to respond to new challenges.

It is difficult to generalise about the profile of teachers, especially internationally, since patterns vary from one country to another. Figure 2.1 shows, for a number of teacher characteristics, the distribution of country experiences. The precise numbers are given in the data appendix; these summary graphs suffice to show the *range* of teacher characteristics by country. The present picture confirms the findings of a 1990 review,[2] which warned against excessive generalisation about teachers and teaching. In particular, the idea that teacher numbers were in decline, that teaching was mainly feminised and that teaching was an ageing profession were found to be simplifications or exaggerations.

Today, as can be seen in Part A of Figure 2.1, school teachers do indeed constitute a substantial percentage of the total employed labour force, but this proportion varies greatly from under 2 to over 4 per cent. The size of the teaching force is a key factor in relation to a number of policy issues, including those of financial resources, since compensation to teachers accounts on average for about two-thirds of current expenditure on primary and secondary education in OECD countries. The cost of education reform is also bound to be influenced by the need to introduce change among a very large number of teachers. Moreover, in considering the size of the education sector it should be borne in mind that the 3 per cent average covers neither personnel outside the school sector nor non-teaching staff within it. Including these categories, an average of over 5 per cent of the employed population is engaged in education (in countries for which such data are available), making it one of the largest single "industrial" sectors.

Figure 2.1 confirms, secondly, a finding of the 1990 review that the level of "feminisation" of teaching varies greatly both by country and by level of education within countries. While many teachers are women, and they dominate the profession in pre-primary and primary schools – in some countries (such as Italy), overwhelmingly so – at secondary level the sexes are in fairly even balance, and in some cases women are the minority. For upper secondary teachers, alongside a small number of countries where women

---

2. OECD(1990). Certain developments relating to teachers have been subject to OECD analysis over the intervening period (eg. OECD,1996*b* and 1997*b*). Comparable data remain limited, though in some areas, such as age of teachers, improvements are imminent.

Figure 2.1
National variations in selected teacher characteristics, 1995

A. Teachers in primary and secondary education as a % of the total labour force (18 countries)

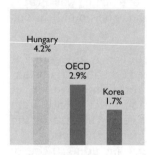

B. Percentage of women among teaching staff

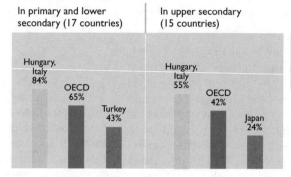

The profile of teacher characteristics varies greatly from one country to another.

C. Ratio of experienced teachers' salary in lower secondary education to GDP per capita (19 countries)

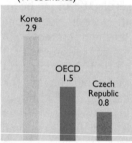

D. Percentage of younger and older teachers in primary and secondary education (13 countries)

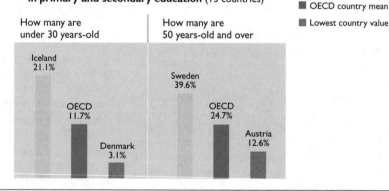

Highest country value
OECD country mean
Lowest country value

Sources: OECD Education Database and Eurydice (1997).
Data for Figure 2.1: *page* 77.

represent over half of the full-time teaching forces (Italy and Hungary), are those countries with reported data where the balance is either very even (New Zealand, Spain, Austria, United States) or where men well out-number women. In Japan, Germany and Korea, only a quarter of teachers at this level are women.[3]

A third type of teacher characteristic, about which the OECD has been gathering an increasing range of data through the INES project (on International Indicators of Education Systems), is the conditions under which they are employed. Figure 2.1 reports that experienced teachers' average salaries vary between 0.8 and 2.9 times average GDP per capita. Other data (OECD, 1996a and 1997b) show for example that:

• *Student-teacher ratios* vary, in primary schools, from 1:24 in Ireland, to 1:10 in Italy. Actual class sizes reported by fourth-grade mathematics teachers show that the most frequent range is 21-30 pupils. The exceptions are: Norway, where the majority are in classes of 20 or below; Ireland, New Zealand and Japan, where 31-40 is the most common size, and

3. The OECD data refer to full-time teachers only, hence some modification might be expected by including part-timers. In some countries, this is not significant: countries with sizeable numbers of part-time teachers tend to be either, such as Germany and the Netherlands, with relatively low rates of feminisation to start with, or else are the Scandanavian examples (Denmark and Sweden), where men as well as women work part-time in teaching (Eurydice, 1997, p.113). At the same time, norms of what constitutes "part-time" also vary significantly.

Korea, where over two thirds of students are in classes with over 40 children.

- The *amount of time* spent working inside and outside classrooms has been estimated at the lower-secondary level. Swedish teachers are contracted to spend 576 hours per year supplying instruction; in the Netherlands and the United States, teachers spend more than 900 hours in class. On top of this, survey data show that in any one week, mathematics teachers spend an average of between 10 and 17 hours on preparation, marking and other out-of-school activities.

- The *role of the principal* is interpreted very differently from one country to another. The position of the principal in the school has an important effect on the teacher's job, in terms of how he or she relates to management. Wide variations in school size means that the average number of teachers managed by a principal ranges, at primary level, from just eight in Norway to 100 in Portugal. Moreover, Portuguese principals spend two-thirds of their time teaching, whereas Norwegian ones spend three-quarters on non-teaching activity. In some countries such as Belgium and Italy, principals are primarily managers who spend little or no time teaching.

International indicators have yet to reveal any systematic relationship between teaching conditions and student achievement. This does not mean that such factors do not influence achievement, but rather that the relationships are complex, and can only be fully understood in terms of interactions at the national, sub-national and local levels. No single variable can be seen as the "key" that unlocks enhanced educational attainment. In general, therefore, the characteristics of teachers and their working conditions across OECD countries can help inform policies towards teachers, but only in tandem with knowledge about the particularities of each country. This is particularly true of the most frequently-cited generalisation about teachers: the "ageing" phenomenon.

EU data (Eurydice, 1997) show that in the majority of European region countries the age profile of teachers is skewed towards the older half of their age range. But patterns vary greatly, as shown in Part D of Figure 2.1: the representation of the over-50s varies within Europe from 39.6 per cent of the teacher population in Sweden to 12.6 per cent in Austria; the under-30s vary in proportion from 21.1 per cent in Iceland to 3.1 per cent in Denmark. Within the older half of the population there is an important distinction between an over-representation of 40-50 year-olds, which exists in most countries, and a large number of over-50s, which is particularly marked in Germany, Italy, Sweden and Norway. The former case primarily raises issues of in-service training; the latter of replacing a large retiring cohort. The ageing phenomenon is especially marked in secondary compared with primary education: in the former, well over a quarter of teachers in the EU are aged 50 years and above (28 per cent), and over two-thirds are 40 or over.

The exact distribution of teacher ages needs to be understood in relation to a number of possible causal factors, including rates of early departures, inflow of young teachers, inflow of mid-career joiners or "returners" and outflows of experienced teachers into non-teaching posts or out of education altogether. But countries' underlying concern is related in large part to whether supply (and, in particular, supply of *good* teachers) can be maintained in the event of large numbers of older teachers reaching retirement age and leaving schools. The above figures do little to allay this concern, especially as regards secondary education. Yet it would be misleading to regard this issue merely as a crisis of recruitment. The "renewal" of teacher competence needs to be considered across the age-range. For teaching forces with large numbers aged in their forties, the issue is how to adapt to the attitudes and technologies of the 21st century. More broadly, there is an issue in societies with ageing populations about how to support and take advantage of maturity and professional experience, and to use them to foster greater stability.

4. THE ROLE OF TEACHER PROFESSIONAL DEVELOPMENT

The key role of training during teachers' service, beyond the initial preparation phase, has come to be widely acknowledged. The age profiles cited above indicate that in most OECD countries the majority of teachers serving in 1998 are likely to have received their initial training before 1980. But this is not the only, nor even the main reason why continuing training and development is a high priority – the more compelling reasons apply equally to younger as to older staff.

In particular, the speed of reform and scale of the expectations for schooling continue to increase, placing new responsibilities on all teachers, and with it the requirement for on-going professional learning. As in other high-skill professional occupations, the pace of change means that continual updating of knowledge and skills is required. Relatedly, recognition of and opportunities for training are important means of enhancing professional status, which does not depend only on tangible benefits such as salary levels.[4] The need for updating is most obvious for those who come into teaching from other backgrounds or after a period out of the profession, and hence it is also an important aspect of enhancing the flexibility of the teaching force in OECD countries; but in fact it applies to all teachers. Equally, in line with other high-skill organisations, the role of professional learning is a key ingredient of the dynamism of schools.

Recognising the force of all these arguments, a recent CERI review of developments in eight countries[5] (OECD, 1998) adopts the concept of "professional development" to signify a broader set of activities than "in-service education and training" (INSET). Organised education and training activities constitute only one, albeit vital, form of professional development. In those schools that have become learning organisations, much development takes place informally with and through colleagues, in many forms. Policy strategies therefore need to look more widely than sending teachers on courses.

The CERI review mentioned above is critical of much of the professional development that in practice takes place, while noting some shift from individual career-oriented training towards whole school developmental activities:

> "There is, of course, no shortage of in-service training in many of the Member countries of the OECD. There is also some evidence of

an emerging paradigm shift from individual to whole school development, driven partly by decentralisation and by increased responsibility on schools to decide their own needs. However, much of what passes for professional development is fragmented and fleeting. All too often it is not focused sufficiently and is too 'top-down' to give teachers any real sense of ownership. It is rarely seen as a continuing enterprise for teachers and it is only occasionally truly *developmental.*" (*op. cit.*, p. 17)

There are many examples of professional learning that is innovative and effective (see Box 2.1). But the finding in the eight countries studied, that too little in-service professional learning by teachers is experienced as a continuing developmental activity linked to broader strategies, puts a question-mark over the future of school reform. Efforts could well be jeopardised by under-investment in the human skills and resources most central to the success of the learning enterprises of schools – those of the teachers.

This analysis is supported by European data from the earlier 1990s (Eurydice, 1995) showing how few resources out of the total education budget are spent on in-service training. In none of the European countries supplying data was the INSET share higher than 2 per cent – in Norway it stood at around this level – and in some cases it is a small fraction of 1 per cent.

These visible training costs are useful in suggesting that investment in serving staff does not yet enjoy high political priority. But figures on spending on formal courses need to be regarded with caution. Countries that succeed in integrating professional learning into the day-to-day life of schools will face lower visible costs in terms of course fees and substitution of teachers absent

---

4. As underscored by the joint ILO/UNESCO experts on the status of teachers: "Whilst improved salaries, better physical facilities and lower class ratios have important impacts, the critical features required to raise the image and self-esteem of teachers in the immediate future include more relevant professional training for individual teachers and improved working conditions and work organisation in schools" (ILO/UNESCO, 1997, p. 10).

5. Germany, Ireland, Japan, Luxembourg, Sweden, Switzerland, United Kingdom, United States.

BOX 2.1 **PROFESSIONAL LEARNING OF TEACHERS**

Work experience for teachers in private companies in Japan

Keidanren, the Japanese employers' association, has produced an *Action Agenda for Reform in Education and Corporate Conduct* that is highly critical of the lack of individuality and creativity in Japanese education and society. A central feature is teacher development: *"If we are to facilitate the development of creative children it is essential that we first enhance the creativity of their teachers"*. With this aim in mind, Keidanren has expanded a programme, run jointly with the Japan Teacher Union, to give teachers experience in industry. Over 60 companies give three-day placements to over 500 teachers during the summer holidays.

Evaluation by the teachers and companies has produced positive responses, although both sides report a "culture shock", and many teachers ask to repeat the experience. Teachers and principals see the benefits as a broadening of teacher perspectives, and an increase in confidence in communication with parents and students. The teachers were particularly impressed by the focus on individual needs in company training systems and by the attention to customers' particular requirements. In retrospect, several were critical of aspects of their initial teacher training which they found by contrast too abstract and top-down.

Local District 2, New York City, United States

This school district is one of the few to create a concerted strategy for using professional development of teachers to bring about system-wide changes in instruction. A strong, determined superintendent appointed in 1987 created a common ethos among teachers and administrators, based around a set of organising principles for systemic change and a set of specific activities or models of staff development.

Professional development is based mainly in the classroom, on the principle that changes in instruction occur only when teachers receive more or less continuous supervision and support focused on the practical details of what it means to teach effectively. One feature is a system of "visiting teachers" with particular learning priorities spending time participating in the classroom of a designated "Resident" teacher. The district also invests in professional development consultants who work intensively with individuals and groups of teachers to tackle specified instructional problems. Peer networking and off-site training also play a role, but summer programmes without follow-up during the school year are not considered helpful.

Source: OECD (1998).

for study. So other evidence, including on the ways in which teachers spend their time within schools, needs to be considered.[6]

As well as seeking to ensure that professional development is oriented to lasting improvements in the work of teachers and schools, policy makers need to consider how to balance potentially competing requirements of teacher learning. Some argue that constant reform diverts too many scarce resources into learning about new requirements or curricula rather than improving profes-

sional practice or raising teacher quality.[7] Must there be trade-offs between updating teachers to

6. For example some estimates suggest that professional development for teachers in Japan amounts to the equivalent of 8 per cent of the school year; a very large share of this time is devoted to on-site, collaborative development activities (Wagner, 1994).

7. "The bulk of INSET provision relates to priorities set nationally and keeps teachers updated about recent reforms, in particular in the curriculum. This has hindered personal development and the continuing development of teaching practices and strategies" (NCE, 1993, p. 219).

realise reform, providing education and training for individuals' career development, and facilitating learning activities organised among colleagues in individual schools or networks of schools? These three important objectives can potentially be complementary rather than mutually exclusive. Individual career enhancement, for instance, might be realised through the acquisition of skills relating to national reforms and through participation in school-level developmental policies. The New York district case example suggests such integrated strategies are possible, with in-service education and training providing a key element within a broader pursuit of improvement that seeks to involve all "players".

So the professional development of teachers will only be effective if it builds on classroom and school practices, which in turn relate closely to organisational and pedagogical strategies. Training is not a linear process of "topping teachers up" to meet their new responsibilities. Expectations relating to in-service training can be at once excessively ambitious and too limited: it is expecting too much of training by itself to enact genuine school improvement; it is expecting too little to use it for limited objectives that are not embedded in larger, dynamic change strategies. It is therefore important in any discussion of teacher roles to consider wider organisational changes that may be needed to create settings in which teacher development can be effective.

5. **BREAKING THE CLASSROOM MOULD?**

The common image of a teacher remains that of the individual professional in a classroom, teaching to her students. More flexible modes of school learning and open structures have often been advocated as the way ahead, necessarily with implications for the work, competences, and practice of teachers. To what extent are schools and school systems willing to break the traditional classroom mould?

There are numerous individual examples of innovative practice and active forms of teaching and learning (as reported in the OECD/Japan seminar held in Hiroshima in 1997, entitled "Schooling for Tomorrow"; see also OECD, 1994 and Stern and Huber, 1997). However, many educational reforms may not foster more innovative practice; they can even inhibit it. Despite widespread decentralisation, and the removal of formal regulation from the centre, attempts to enforce reform with student assessment, accountability mechanisms, and the monitoring of standards may also remove incentives for some schools and teachers to innovate by pioneering new practices with uncertain outcomes.[8]

While the present state of data gives an unclear picture of the extent of change in classroom models, it is useful to identify ways in which variations are emerging. Three areas are of particular interest: the extent to which teaching takes place among collaborative teams rather than isolated individuals; the involvement in classrooms of adults other than teachers; and the degree to which information and communications technology have transformed classroom practice.

Team teaching

The prevalence of the single-teacher classroom situation is in some cases modified through the adoption of more complex, collaborative models of work by teachers in teams. Some caution is needed over the label "team teaching", which can mean anything from better communication among teachers of children in a year-group to the presence of multiple teachers in individual classrooms. Box 2.2 outlines examples of relevant experiences, at national and school levels so far identified by the OECD. For some schools, and indeed systems, forms of team teaching are now normal practice, and the examples presented are drawn from across the different levels of schooling. However, it is hard at this stage to gauge overall penetration of such practice, which could be a subject of future investigation.

More complex, collaborative models of teaching and the organisation of learning are in general more demanding professionally and call on a wider range of skills and competences than simpler models. With such demands, the room for

8. As expressed by Darling-Hammond (1997): "The concerns of the teachers in our study are precisely those that current reforms are seeking to address, yet many policies unwittingly set up greater prescriptions, which actually undermine the goals they seek" (p. 94).

BOX 2.2 **NATIONAL AND SCHOOL EXAMPLES OF TEAM TEACHING**

• New arrangements were introduced in *Italy* in 1990 as part of a large-scale reform process in primary schools: classes grouped together in twos or threes and taught by two or more teachers. The new system of teaching breaks the traditional "one teacher/one class" approach. In the current school year – 1997-1998 – the majority of pupils (85 per cent) are taught within this new framework.

Normally, a group of three teachers instruct pupils in two classes of the same age, although different age-groups may sometimes be combined in the same class, with teachers sharing responsibility for class work. Primary teachers no longer work as generalists. Subjects are grouped into three broad areas of learning: linguistic-expressive, scientific-logical-mathematical and historical-geographical-social. To assure consistency in teaching, teachers are expected to plan together: there are co-operative planning arrangements and a regular weekly time is scheduled for this purpose.

• In *Viborg Amtsgymnasium Upper Secondary School, Denmark*, tutorial teams of 3-4 teachers of one class cooperate in a particularly close network. The other teachers of the class are informed continuously about special matters pertinent to the class, individual students, pedagogical innovations, etc. These teachers are members of tutorial teams in other classes. All teachers are as a rule members of two tutorial teams in the school and more informally associated with the other classes they teach.

• At *Utase Elementary School, Japan*, teaching is not necessarily conducted on the basis of the single class unit of 30-40 pupils, but normally by means of team teaching combining two classes together. Team teaching makes it easier to adapt various teaching methods such as whole class teaching, individualized study, group learning, etc. to meet varied abilities, progress, needs and preferences of the pupils.

• At *Arnestad School, Norway*, a 1997 reform reorganised the school day and school year, and decentralised decisions about the timetable. So classes have lessons of varying length and breaks at different points of time during the day. The school year is divided into six terms, each with a teaching plan emphasizing different themes or subjects. The Norwegian school curriculum requires teachers to work in teams. At Arnestad a teacher team shares responsibility for the teaching and the follow-up work of pupils in parallel grades.

Source: OECD/Japan seminar held in Hiroshima, November 1997, entitled "Schooling for Tomorrow".

professional frustration can grow when these skills and competences are not exercised; at the same time, the potential for enhanced satisfaction and the removal of individual isolation can bear substantial results. To share the organisation and task of teaching is a more natural step when there is already extensive discussion and planning among teachers concerning other aspects of school life. In-service and initial training play a vital part in preparing teachers for these roles, as do professional development and wider support. If these are not provided or organised, more complex arrangements risk foundering. They may also be opposed by assumptions about the teacher as individual subject expert. Yet, as the Italian example shows, team-teaching, at least at the primary level, may be consistent with more subject specialisation rather than less. How well this holds at the secondary level, especially where traditions of academic specialisation are strong, is another matter.

Involvement of other adults in the classroom

A different set of issues are raised by another source of modification of the single-teacher in the classroom model: the introduction of parents and other adults into teaching situations. A recent CERI study examined the role of parents in schools (OECD, 1997a), and found that while there are numerous positive examples relating to consultative governance and active parental involvement in homework schemes, there is far less evidence of such involvement in school-based teaching and learning. Where it does occur, it is much more at the primary than secondary levels, and involves mainly mothers. It takes place as part of particular programmes to address disadvantage or to bridge school/community divides, and more generally in reading schemes. Such initiatives tend to complement rather than transform mainstream practice.

The issues raised are complex. On the one hand, the involvement of outsiders can open up the otherwise rigid mould of classroom practice. This may take place "from the inside" by accessing parental and other community resources as support in classrooms, or "from the outside" through community-initiated programmes in which learning is not primarily managed by teachers as such. The benefits realised by students participating in such initiatives require further evaluation.

But how far should such outside involvement lead to a redefinition of who can take on the role of teacher? There may well be value in promoting alternative routes into teaching. On the other hand, there is the important risk that the professionalism necessary for high quality teaching and learning will be undermined. Opening up classrooms could encourage the view, notwithstanding extensive contrary evidence, that teaching requires no specialised knowledge and training – the "bright person myth" (Darling-Hammond, 1997, p. 309; and Holmes Group, 1986). U.S. research suggests that "not only is teacher quality the single most important determinant of student performance, but low-income and minority students are least likely to receive instruction from well-qualified, highly effective teachers" (Darling-Hammond and Falk, 1997, p. 192). Key educational and equity principles are at issue.

So it is crucial to stress that opening up class-rooms and teaching is not an alternative to professionalism, and should imply no sacrifice in quality (although "quality" may be defined in broad ways, based on teacher competence and enquiring abilities rather than just qualifications and knowledge). The CERI report on parents (OECD, 1997a) argues that well-planned initiatives can enhance teaching and learning resources and need not lead to de-professionalisation. No single model of outside involvement can be prescribed or avoided. Rather there is a need to identify conditions that promote teacher professionalism and the imperative of quality teaching alongside flexible arrangements that engage both students and the community. In so doing, equity questions need to be taken seriously: how far do innovative practices, involving a mix of more and less traditional teaching and learning resources, typify the high-income, affluent schools, risking simply to widen existing social divides?

ICT *and new learning models*

Perhaps the most commonly-cited factor heralding fundamental change in the structure and organisation of schooling, with profound implications for the teacher, is the spreading impact of information and communication technologies (ICT) on learning. The last full meeting of OECD Education Ministers in 1996 identified as a priority the need to analyse "schooling for tomorrow (…) in particular in the light of new technologies and advances in pedagogy" (OECD, 1996a, p. 24). How important are these developments for the question "who is the teacher?" What role do teachers have – is their importance being diminished by the fact that learning can take place and information accessed in many new ways outside the classroom and away from the direction of the teacher?

As shown in Figure 2.2, the number of computers in schools varies greatly among OECD countries. More important, however, is the fact that many countries are investing heavily to equip schools with computers, Internet connections, software and multi-media. Any static survey is almost instantly out of date: even from one year to another the ratio of students to computers often falls sharply. In the United States, for example, there are wide internal variations,

Figure 2.2
Computers in schools

Average number of students per computer

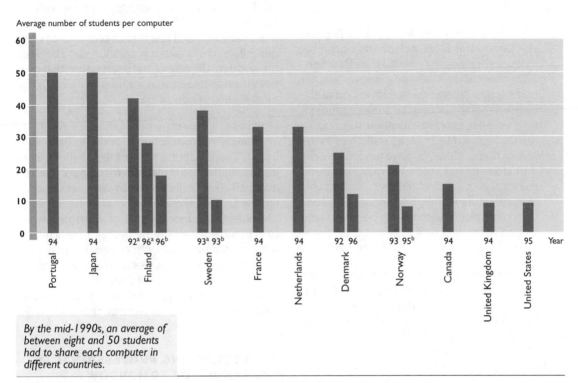

By the mid-1990s, an average of between eight and 50 students had to share each computer in different countries.

a. Primary and lower secondary schools.
b. Upper secondary schools.
Source: OECD (1997*d*).
Data for Figure 2.2: page 77.

from fewer than six students per computer in Florida and Wyoming, to 16 in Louisiana and about 10 nationally in 1995-96 (Coley, 1997, pp. 10-13). Such ratios do not of course tell whether equipment is up-to-date, relevant or well-used. So the same US report estimated that there was only one multi-media computers with CD-Rom capacity for every 25 students.

More fundamental than hardware investment is the manner in which computers are used and the difference this can and does make to the teaching and learning experience. There are many claims made regarding teaching and learning methods that exploit information and communication technologies in schools, yet surprisingly little firm evidence and evaluation is available to support high expectations. Moreover, too little is known about the consequences of computer

use in education. The lack of good, relevant educational software and multi-media is itself a disincentive for use, since teachers, parents and others hesitate to buy software which is of questionable quality, or which does not correspond to the taught curriculum. This in turn inhibits the development of a market for high quality educational software and multi-media, creating a vicious circle.[9]

But it does seem clear that the essential professional support for teachers in making best use of new technologies remains under-developed and under-resourced. The OECD 1997 *Information*

9. Such questions are now being analysed in a new project on "New Developments in Educational Software and Multimedia" as part of the CERI work on "Schooling for Tomorrow."

Technology Outlook summarised evidence from policy reports and research across a range of countries to conclude:

> "Successful deployment and use of ICTs in the classroom still largely depends on highly motivated, pioneering principals and teachers. Although the lack of appropriate teacher training and experience was identified at the beginning of the decade as a major problem for effective use of IT in education, most policy discussions and technology initiatives in the area of IT and education have tended to focus on hardware and software acquisition and students' access to technology (...). Computer literacy is still generally low among educators: the majority lack the necessary training, some lack an appreciation of ICTs and their classroom potential." (OECD, 1997*d*, p. 135)

It is not just a matter of developing appropriate knowledge and skill but of changing attitudes. The teacher is commonly identified as much as a barrier as a key medium, too often defensive and ill-equipped compared with students comfortable with computer applications. One danger is that ICTs are seen as replacing rather than aiding good teaching. IEA (International Association for the Evaluation of Educational Achievement) studies (Plomp *et al.*, 1997) have described not only resistance but the predominantly traditional use of ICT in the classroom as a substitute for conventional pedagogic approaches. The large majority of Swedish school principals, surveyed in 1995, believed the impact of ICTs on students to be significant in relation to such matters as ability to work independently, solve problems, and prepare for working life; fewer than half thought they would have any significant impact on teaching (cited in OECD, 1997*c*, p. 121). Still more clearcut, a 1996 survey of English secondary school heads of subject departments found that, in most subjects, very few believed that ICT was exercising a "substantial" impact on teaching and learning in their schools and departments (although about half thought that it had "some" impact).

A pessimistic scenario might be that technological gulfs too large to be bridged have been created and with far-reaching implications for the relevance of school curricula. The much greater access by the young to complex technologies, whether through networking, electronic games, or multi-media, has, on this view, created wide cognitive and cultural rifts between children and teachers. Others are more sanguine and see this as part of the perennial differences between generations, and between the worlds of the school and peer culture, that need not give rise to alarm, nor undermine the fundamental aims of education.

Whichever scenario turns out to be the more accurate, a key conclusion to underline is that, far from ICT representing an *alternative* to the teacher, its imaginative use is highly demanding of teachers and staff. This is illustrated by case observations reported to the Hiroshima OECD/Japan seminar on "Schooling for Tomorrow", two of which are referred to in Box 2.3. To facilitate active learning is not the same as handing over professional expertise to hardware and software. Rather than diminishing the role of the teacher, ICTs have the potential to enhance it, making possible a more diverse curriculum and a more demanding repertoire for teacher skills and organisation.

6. THE TEACHING PROFESSIONAL IN THE SCHOOL OF TOMORROW

The future role of teachers depends not just on the specifics of how instruction is organised, but on the future position of the school itself. Will it remain a key social institution, or is it set to decline?

Arguments positing a declining role for schools and teachers today and tomorrow prominently include the following inter-related sets of observations:

- The growth of *alternative* sources of information and knowledge means the rapid decline of the monopoly of schools over information and knowledge. The burgeoning of new forms of influence, via media, peer and youth cultures, it is argued, further reduces the impact of what schools have to offer.

- *Globalisation* – economic, political and cultural – is said by some to render obsolete the locally-based, culturally-bounded institution called "school" (and with it the "teacher").

BOX 2.3 **DEMANDING ROLES FOR TEACHERS WITH ICT USE**

"A major lesson learned in this context is that the introduction of the 'study house'* should be extremely well prepared. The teaching methods used in the model require further consideration. There is a strong need for the further development of methods that are appropriate for this new educational concept. This goes particularly for the use of information and communication technologies, including the Internet."

Carolus College, Netherlands

"The innovations at Monkseaton are based on the premise that schools must become learning organizations that will equip students to live and learn in an information society (...). Part of this is the rigorous evaluation of improvements in student attitudes and achievement. To do this, Monkseaton is creating a new learning environment that combines the best of traditional teaching and learning with:

– Lifelong learning skills and attitudes;

– Appropriate technology, especially communications and information technologies;

– Access to the new learning environment in school and at home;

– Partnerships with industry, the community, and students themselves."

Monkseaton Community High School, England

---

* A model of independent learning being introduced in some schools in the Netherlands through national policy.

- Even within schools, the greater *individualisation* of modes of learning – flexible, demand-driven – might be seen as displacing cumbersome, supply-dominated models. This heralds the corresponding decline of teachers, further signalled by the growth of alternative sources of learning, including through ICT and through human resources other than teachers.

But must these influences weaken schools and teachers? Not necessarily. It would be a great oversimplification to regard schools as being exclusively about the transmission of knowledge and conclude that this task can now simply be transferred to computers. Schools have always had wider roles, including social functions, which are now likely to become more rather than less important. With the weakening of institutions such as the family and the local community, for example, the socialisation of young people becomes simultaneously more important and more difficult: some would like to see the school as a social linchpin of otherwise fragmented, individualised societies (Carnoy and

Castells, 1997). Similarly, they may provide a local locus in a confusingly globalised world. It would also be wrong to exaggerate the degree to which schools in the past have had a monopoly of knowledge: families, churches, and communities have always played a role, if anything more strongly before than now; broadcasting has been influential for over half a century.

In some respects, therefore, the assumed tasks of the school have been extended, perhaps unrealistically, rather than superceded. Whether schools can start to meet these expectations will depend to a high degree on their ability to develop a central position in society, as more "open" organisations serving a wide range of interests and clientele.

There is thus no inevitability about a weakening role for schools in the light of some of the major changes taking place that impact on them, and they may on the contrary lead to a reinvigorated and still stronger institution. These same trends could well, however, be creating tensions that are extremely hard to accommodate within existing systems. Which way it turns out is crucially dependent on what teachers do collectively, and how they are permitted to develop their schools, separately and across systems. It also depends on whether they can define a new type of professionalism that is central, rather than supplementary, to the ways in which learning takes place.

This new professionalism will need to draw from both old and new models of what it means to be a good teacher. Most importantly it will require:

- *Expertise*. This traditional characteristic of the good teacher will not be the only attribute needed, but its importance should not therefore be under-estimated. It has been demonstrated that a good teacher needs to be an important source of knowledge and understanding. However, the way in which teachers themselves access knowledge needs to change: there should be less reliance on initial training and more on continuous updating.

- *Pedagogical know-how* also continues to be essential, but again in a changing context. In a framework of lifelong learning, teachers have to become competent at transmitting a range of high-level skills including motivation to learn, creativity and co-operation, rather than placing too high a premium on information recall or performance in tests.

- **Understanding of technology** is a new key feature of teacher professionalism. Most important is an understanding of its pedagogical potential, and an ability to integrate it into teaching strategies rather than leaving students to learn from self-contained programmes as a separate process.

- *Organisational competence and collaboration.* Teacher professionalism can no longer be seen simply as an individualised competence, but rather must incorporate the ability to function as part of a "learning organisation". The ability and willingness to learn from and to teach other teachers is perhaps the most important aspect of this attribute.

- *Flexibility* is an attribute of teacher professionalism which perhaps conflicts most

directly with traditional notions. Teachers have to accept that professional requirements may change several times in the course of their careers, and not interpret professionalism as an excuse to resist change.

- *Mobility* is desirable for some if not all teachers: the capacity and willingness to move in and out of other careers and experiences that will enrich their abilities as teachers.

- *Openness* is another skill for many teachers to learn: being able to work with parents and other non-teachers in ways that complement rather than subvert other aspects of the teacher's professional role is perhaps the most challenging way in which notions of professionalism can be adapted.

7. CONCLUSIONS

In short, this new type of professionalism challenges teachers to function in learning organisations committed to laying the foundations of lifelong learning. The above list of characteristics is not a "static" description of who can be recognised as a professional teacher, but a set of attributes that need to be developed in a continued learning process.

So it is not just inputs, in terms of numbers and qualifications of teachers, nor outcomes in terms of measurable student achievement, that make good schools. Giving attention to the *processes* of teaching and learning brings human and professional endeavours to the fore. A focus on process may appear inward-looking, but can potentially raise challenging and uncomfortable questions about what happens in many schools. Classroom doors will be opened to scrutiny, rather than letting teachers "get on with" a business that only they know best. An intense attention to process may well expose precisely how prevalent "industrial" input-output models of the learning process remain in some schools in OECD countries, and bring pressure for improvement.

The new teacher professionalism will be highly demanding, supplementing traditional requirements with new ones. It remains to be seen how far the relevant stakeholders – including governments, parents, the general public and teachers themselves – are ready to invest in and embrace such professionalism. ■

References

CARNOY, M. and **CASTELLS, M**. (1997), "Sustainable flexibility: A prospective study on work, family and society in the information age", Free Document, Centre for Educational Research and Innovation, OECD, Paris.

COLEY, R.J. (1997), *Computers and Classrooms: The Status of Technology in US Schools*, ETS, Princeton.

DARLING-HAMMOND, L. (1997), *The Right to Learn: A Blueprint for Creating Schools that Work*, Jossey Bass, San Francisco.

DARLING-HAMMOND, L. and **FALK, B.** (1997), "Using standards and assessments to support student learning", *Phi Delta Kappan*, November.

DEPARTMENT FOR EDUCATION AND EMPLOYMENT – DfEE (1997), "Survey of information technology use in schools 1996", *Statistical Bulletin*, No. 3/97, UK Stationery Office, Norwich, March.

EURYDICE (1995), *In-service Training of Teachers in the European Union and the EFTA/EEA Countries*, EC, Brussels.

EURYDICE (1996), *A Decade of Reforms at Compulsory Education Level in the European Union (1984-94)*, EC, Brussels.

EURYDICE (1997), *Key Data on Education in the European Union*, EC, Luxembourg.

HOLMES GROUP (1986), *Tomorrow's Teachers: A Report of the Holmes Group*, East Lansing, MI.

ILO/UNESCO (1997), *Joint ILO/UNESCO Committee of Experts on the Application of the Recommendation Concerning the Status of Teachers*, Special Fourth Session, Paris, September.

NATIONAL COMMISSION FOR EDUCATION – NCE (1993), *Learning to Succeed: A Radical Look at Education Today and a Strategy for the Future*, Report of the Paul Hamlyn Foundation, Heinemann, London.

OECD (1990), *The Teacher Today: Tasks, Conditions, Policies*, Paris.

OECD (1994), *Quality in Teaching*, Paris.

OECD (1995), *Public Expectations of the Final Stage of Compulsory Education*, Paris.

OECD (1996a), *Lifelong Learning for All*, Paris.

OECD (1996b), *Education at a Glance: Analysis*, Chapter 4 "Teachers Pay and Conditions", Paris.

OECD (1997a), *Parents as Partners in Schooling*, "What Works in Innovation in Education" series, Paris.

OECD (1997b), *Education at a Glance: OECD Indicators 1997*, Chapters B "Financial and human resources invested in education" and D "The learning environment and the organisation of schools", Paris.

OECD (1997c), "Demand for Internet-based services: Education, business services and entertainment", Free document, DSTI/ICCP/IE(97)9, Paris.

OECD (1997d), *Information Technology Outlook 1997*, Chapter 8 "ICT as a tool for lifelong learning", Paris.

OECD (1998), *Staying Ahead: In-service Training and Teacher Professional Development*, "What Works in Innovation in Education" series, Paris.

PLOMP, T., BRUMMELHUIS, A. T. and **PELGRUM, W.J.** (1997), "New approaches for teaching, learning and using information and communication technologies in education", *Prospects*, Vol. XXVII, No. 3.

STERN, D. and **HUBER, G.L.** (Eds.) (1997), *Active Learning for Students and Teachers: Reports from Eight Countries*, OECD and Peter Lang, Frankfurt am Main.

UNESCO (1998), *World Education Report 1998 – Teachers and Teaching in a Changing World*, Paris.

VILLEGAS-REIMARS, E. and **REIMERS, F.** (1996), "Where are the missing 60 million teachers? The missing voice in educational reforms around the world", *Prospects*, Vol. XXVI, No. 3.

WAGNER, A. (1994), "The economics of teacher education", in Tuijnman, A. and Postlethwaite, N. (Eds), *The International Encyclopaedia of Education*, Pergamon Press, Oxford.

CHAPTER 3

SUPPORTING YOUTH PATHWAYS

SUMMARY

Many young people face serious difficulties in progressing from education into work. While policy responses have not eliminated such problems, they have not universally failed either. A more precise understanding is needed of what has worked to support youth pathways in the past, and what can help in the future.

The *supply* of youth labour varies considerably across countries in terms of both cohort sizes and the proportion who lack qualifications. On the *demand* side, the labour market is now generally less favourable to the unqualified, but this bias is not equally strong everywhere. Among OECD countries, the proportion of young adults without upper-secondary education who are unemployed varies from 3 to 30 per cent. There is no consistent relationship between the proportion who are unqualified and their relative employment chances. The strongest employment growth is in the service sector. Although some service jobs can favour young people who have a sound general education and good computing and language skills, there are also many low-skill jobs where young people are over-represented and overqualified.

How quickly young people find their first job after leaving school has a powerful effect on their subsequent employment experiences. During the first five years on the labour market, there are wide variations in experience by country and gender. Young American women who leave school early spend only a third of this period in work, compared to seven-eighths for young German men.

So policy needs to focus on the pathways young people follow after leaving school. Some countries offer more stable and sometimes rigid routes, others more open and sometimes fragile ones. The former model has tended to have more success in helping young people to get into their first job, and limiting long-term unemployment.

However, in developing future policy options, international experience suggests no single approach but the need to combine strong stable structures with flexible pathways to suit individual needs. The conditions in many countries are not appropriate for German-style apprenticeships. But two other policy options are worth considering. One is to extend the use of "double-qualifying" pathways – upper secondary programmes that can lead either directly into the labour market or to tertiary education. The other is to develop more comprehensive and coherent opportunities, both before and after leaving school, to create a "youth guarantee" in the style of Nordic countries.

Key features of all these strategies are to focus first and foremost on reducing failure at school, so that subsequent measures can be targeted at a relatively small number, and to ensure that education, labour market and social policies operate in complementary ways.

1. INTRODUCTION

The problems facing people in their late teens and early 20s are high on the policy agenda in OECD countries. There is particular concern that significant numbers of young people do not succeed in education, have trouble in gaining stable employment and face social and economic marginalisation.

There is a common perception that youth policy measures have not succeeded. But concerns about current youth problems and the assumption that past policies have failed are often based on rather broad and ambiguous evidence. A more precise, objective analysis of the situation facing today's young adults shows that their situation is highly variable, and that certain policies have indeed helped them.

This chapter presents an overview of:

- the context in which young people come onto the labour market;
- the change in the employment opportunities that they encounter when they get there;
- the different pathways that they take in moving from education into work; and
- the policy measures that have most effectively helped them to do so.

This analysis considers the importance to young people of educational outcomes and of labour market conditions, but also draws attention to the dynamics of the transition from education to employment. Young people must follow often lengthy, individualised pathways between full-time education and full integration into work and adult society. The structure and level of support that they get in this process is a key policy issue, even though overall, policy needs to give high priority to reducing the risk of failure in education itself.

2. YOUNG PEOPLE ENTERING THE LABOUR MARKET

In most OECD countries, compulsory schooling finishes at the age of 15 or 16 years. But transition to the labour market takes place over a wide span of ages, typically from the late teens to the mid-twenties.[1] Youth policy is therefore commonly directed to approximately the 15-24 age group, while recognising that many problems related to

social and economic integration have their roots much earlier in the education and social systems.

Two general characteristics of the youth population help to set the context of their experiences: their numbers and their education levels. These factors influence the "supply side" of the labour market.

Cohort sizes

About 160 million of the 1.1 billion people in the OECD's 29 Member countries are aged between 15 and 24. This youth cohort shrank by about 3 per cent in the ten years to 1998, but the countries varied widely around the average. In some there was a big drop – of around 20 per cent or more in Denmark, Germany, Italy, the Netherlands, Norway and the United Kingdom. On the other hand, the youth cohort grew appreciably in the Czech Republic, Hungary, Mexico, Poland and Turkey. Overall it is forecast to decline by a further 4 per cent by 2008.

Even more striking than country differences in trends in youth numbers is the variation in the youth share of the total population. Just 9 per cent of Swiss people and around 12 per cent of the Belgian, Danish, German, Dutch, Norwegian, Swedish and United Kingdom populations are aged 15-24. This contrasts with 18 per cent in Ireland and over 20 per cent in Mexico and Turkey. Figure 3.1 shows that in almost all cases, countries with higher than average income per head have smaller than average youth populations, and vice versa. In principle this permits the former to spend more per capita on services for young people – subject to their ordering of spending priorities. It also implies that the relatively low-income countries face particular difficulties in meeting the needs of their young people.

The size of the youth cohort can influence on the one hand the resources that governments spend on initial education and training and, on the other, the competition that young people face for entry-level jobs. Where the youth population is shrinking, there may be pressure on governments

---

1. On average in OECD countries, a quarter of the population leave education, or mix it with work, by the age of 17, and the majority are in work but not studying by the age of 23: see OECD (1996a), *Education at a Glance - Analysis*, p. 45.

Figure 3.1
Youth population and GDP per capita

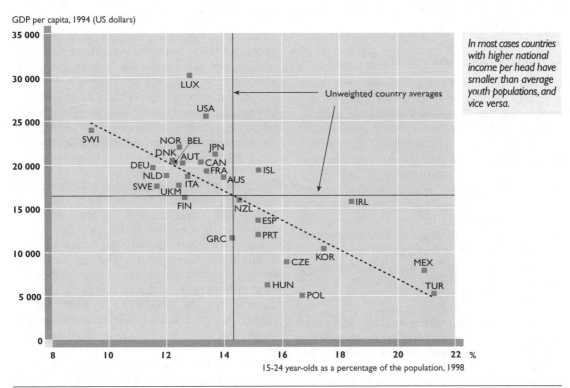

GDP per capita, 1994 (US dollars)

In most cases countries with higher national income per head have smaller than average youth populations, and vice versa.

15-24 year-olds as a percentage of the population, 1998

Sources: Projections based on the United Nations population database and OECD (1997a).
Data for Figure 3.1: page 78.

to reduce overall education and training expenditure, especially where there is growth in the retired population, which pushes up pension and healthcare costs. However, where education spending is maintained or not reduced proportionately to the fall in youth numbers, per capita spending on young people will rise. Norway, for example, took advantage of such a "demographic dividend" to fund reforms to upper secondary education that were introduced in 1994. Demands on government spending on youth services are a function not only of the cohort's size but also of its composition. The needs are likely to be greater, for example, in countries where the youth cohort contains a high proportion of recently arrived migrants, or groups disadvantaged by social background or geography.

The degree to which young people in small cohorts benefit from reduced competition for jobs is influenced by what is happening elsewhere on the labour market. The overall age structure of the population and employment practices with respect to older workers are significant. Potentially, young people can be better placed to obtain jobs where youth are relatively few in number. The danger in this situation is that easier immediate job prospects may encourage a long-term under-investment in skills, which would harm the economy. Conversely a larger youth population, combined with effective educational investment and the removal of barriers to youth employment, can invigorate the labour market through an increasing number of new entrants with enthusiasm and fresh, relevant skills.

However, the effect of demographic factors on young people's transition to work should not be over-emphasised. Despite declines in the size of the youth cohort in most OECD countries, and strong growth in sectors that employ large numbers of young people (such as retail trade, hospitality and tourism), the relative employment and earnings positions of young people have tended to decline between the mid-1980s and the mid-1990s (OECD, 1996*b*).

Low qualification levels

A major preoccupation of policy makers is those who lack educational qualifications. Young people who face the greatest risks are those who struggle in education from an early age and have at the most limited and intermittent engagement with further learning after the minimum leaving age. Educational attainment is becoming increasingly important, relative to other factors, in shaping young people's life chances. Research shows that the direct influence of factors like social class, ethnicity and gender on economic and social success is declining. These factors remain important, but their impact is increasingly operating via their influence on access to, and success in, education.

The main focus of concern is on those who enter the labour market directly from secondary school, especially those who lack qualifications either for further study or access to an apprenticeship place or a job. (The particular problems faced by the high proportion of disabled young people who lack post-compulsory qualifications are discussed in OECD, 1997*c*.) The propensity to leave school before completing upper secondary education relates to available job opportunities, but also to social factors, to individual attitudes towards education, and to the structure of linkages between education and the labour market.

The influence of these factors varies among countries. In Australia, for example, research indicates that young people leave school early mainly because they dislike its atmosphere and content, and despite the fact that unemployment among early school leavers is very high. In Portugal, by contrast, those who leave without upper secondary qualifications are actually less likely to be unemployed than the better-qualified. It seems that the Portuguese labour market is still able to absorb young people with low levels of formal qualifications, although the country does experience a relatively high rate of emigration of lower-skilled young workers.

There is concern, though, about the long-term prospects of such young people in an increasingly dynamic economy.

As shown in Figure 3.2, the proportion of young people who have not completed upper secondary education is still substantial in many countries, although there is wide variation. On average, almost one in four (24 per cent) of 20-24 year-olds lack qualifications beyond the end of compulsory schooling – ranging from over one in two in Turkey and Portugal to less than one in ten in Norway, the Czech Republic and Korea.

The number of young people without upper secondary qualifications has been declining across OECD countries during the 1990s, but unevenly. In some countries that began the decade with particularly high numbers of unqualified young adults, the fall has been striking – by the equivalent of one-third of the total cohort in Ireland and Portugal, and one quarter in Italy, from 1989 to 1995. But in countries with relatively well-qualified young people in 1989, the fall has been more modest.

One interesting feature of this population of young adults with low qualifications is that in most countries it is composed unevenly of men and women – but the imbalance is not always in the same direction (see data for Figure 3.2 in the statistical annex, p.78). In nine countries, at least 5 per cent more of the young male population than of the young female population has low qualifications. In five countries the reverse applies. Measures to reform school curricula and teaching approaches, as well as measures to change general social attitudes, have been attempted to ensure that early school leavers are not concentrated along gender lines. These have yet to be effective in many countries. It is apparent, however, that there is a strong relationship between the incidence of low qualifications and the extent of gender differences. Where very few young people have low qualifications, the difference between males and females in the extent to which each group possesses low qualifications is low. Where very many young people emerge from education with low qualifications, the differences in attainment levels between males and females are likely to be considerable.

Figure 3.2
Young people with low educational qualifications
Percentage of 20-24 year-olds whose highest level of educational attainment is lower secondary school, 1989 and 1995

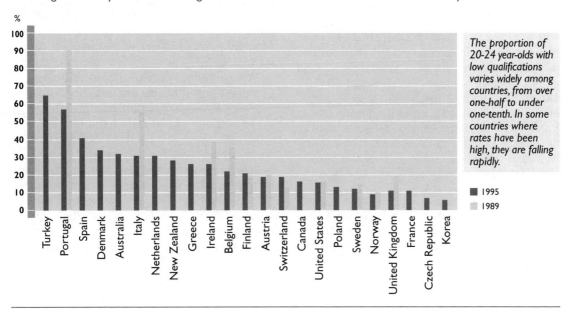

The proportion of 20-24 year-olds with low qualifications varies widely among countries, from over one-half to under one-tenth. In some countries where rates have been high, they are falling rapidly.

■ 1995
■ 1989

Source: OECD Education Database.
Data for Figure 3.2: *page* 78.

3. CHANGING EMPLOYMENT OPPORTUNITIES

Although not all youth policy issues revolve around the labour market, the problems associated with finding and holding jobs should not be underestimated. Among other things, the difficulty of finding work can lead to excessively extended periods in formal education and prolonged dependency. Difficulties in finding a job during the period immediately after leaving school can have a significant impact on the chances of young people settling into the labour market in the succeeding years.

Nearly all OECD countries experienced falling participation in employment by young people between the mid-1980s and the mid-1990s. The proportion in employment fell from 44 per cent to 35 per cent of 18-year-olds, and from 68 per cent to 59 per cent of 22-year-olds (OECD, 1996a). Much of this reduction can be explained by falling labour force participation as the result of rising educational participation. But young people's employment opportunities are changing in other ways. For example, in many countries it is now

more common than previously to combine work with study, and to do this other than through traditional pathways such as apprenticeship. In Australia, Canada, Denmark, the Netherlands, the United Kingdom and the United States, 20 per cent or more of all 16-19 year-old students are also workers (OECD, 1996a).

In some countries concern is expressed at the growing incidence of involuntary part time, temporary or other forms of insecure employment by young people once they leave full-time education, although the extent of this is not easy to measure. It is clear, however, that in some countries the extended periods spent by school leavers in part-time and temporary employment as well as unemployment can have negative effects on longer-term careers (OECD, 1998b).

Although this complex new youth labour market defies simple description, three relevant features are analysed below: the job prospects of young people with low qualifications; the actual experiences of this group in the years immediately after leaving school; and changes in the industries in which young people are working.

Prospects for the poorly-qualified

In virtually all OECD countries young people are entering labour markets in which the level of demanded skills and qualifications is rising, and where those without marketable skills or recognised qualifications find it increasingly difficult to compete for work. Data from a group of 14 countries, spanning the 1980s and 1990s, shows that in the labour force as a whole employment among those with no more than a lower secondary level of education declined at an average rate of 2 per cent a year, amounting to a substantial total change over the decade (OECD, 1997b).

Figure 3.2 above showed that the proportion of young people with no more than lower-secondary education varies widely among countries. Figure 3.3 shows that the disadvantage that this

confers is also highly variable: in Finland, France, Ireland, Italy and Spain about a quarter or more of poorly qualified young adults were unemployed in 1995; in Austria and Korea, only 6 per cent or less. How does the size of the unqualified population affect the prospects of its members? On the one hand educational norms can affect employers' attitudes to low qualifications: if having a high school diploma or a vocational qualification becomes the norm, those without one seem all the less employable. This seems to be the case in countries such as France where only around 10 per cent of 20-24 year-olds have low qualifications, and high levels of general unemployment mean that they face strong competition for jobs. On the other hand, the availability of unskilled jobs will affect the prospects of the unqualified. If the pool of such jobs is limited, a large supply of

Figure 3.3
Young people with low qualifications: proportion of age-group and chances of being unemployed
Percentage of 20-24 year-olds whose highest level of educational attainment is lower secondary school, and percentage of this low attainment group who are unemployed, 1995

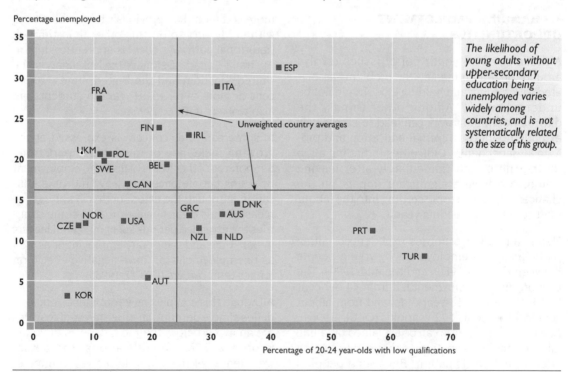

Percentage unemployed

The likelihood of young adults without upper-secondary education being unemployed varies widely among countries, and is not systematically related to the size of this group.

Percentage of 20-24 year-olds with low qualifications

Source: OECD Education Database.
Data for Figure 3.3: page 78.

unqualified young people might make it hard for each individual to compete for the available work. However, if such jobs are more plentiful, as appears to be the case in a country like Portugal, the problems of job seekers with low qualifications will be reduced somewhat.

Overall, there appears to be no systematic relationship between the proportion of less-educated young people (shown on the horizontal axis of Figure 3.3) and their likelihood of being unemployed. So for example the 31 per cent of young adults with low educational attainment in Italy were three times as likely to be unemployed as the 31 per cent of low-qualified young adults in the Netherlands. The same applies for pairs of countries where the rates of low educational attainment were below average; for example, French 20-24 year-olds without upper-secondary education were twice as likely to be unemployed as Norwegian ones.

So the variation in the fortunes of the low-qualified is not purely a function of their numbers: other explanations must be sought. One interesting observation is that most of the countries in which those with low qualifications suffer the least unemployment place strong emphasis on young people obtaining recognised vocational qualifications immediately after the end of compulsory schooling. This is true of Austria, the Netherlands and Norway, which are also countries in which employers and trade unions are actively involved with government in setting the curriculum and certification frameworks for such qualifications, and in negotiating their labour market value. An intriguing question is why, in countries that place a high value on coherent qualifications for employment, young people without such qualifications should have low unemployment rates.

Making a start in the job market

Given that employers use both qualifications and experience to select workers, early school leavers are at a double disadvantage. They tend to spend a relatively long time searching for a first job and they are more likely to end up with work of poor quality. Although low-pay jobs can be a stepping stone to better employment, the evidence suggests that such jobs are often only temporary,

and that especially the unqualified young person soon returns to the unemployment pool.

Yet not all those who leave school before completing upper secondary education are necessarily at risk in the labour market. The greatest problems face those who do not subsequently enrol in further education, and who are unemployed or outside the labour force altogether. What happens in the first year after leaving school is particularly important. Longitudinal data analysed for Australia, France, Germany, Ireland and the United States (OECD, 1998b) indicate that young people who are either unemployed or outside the labour force in the first year after leaving education spend substantially less time in work over the following five years than those who find work early. For example:

- Young men in the United States who do not complete high school, but find a job in their first year after leaving, spend on average 85 per cent of the following four years working. But those who find no job in the first year work only 50 per cent of the next four.

- Young women spend on average less time working than men during the years after leaving school – especially if they are not qualified. The gap between male and female employment rates is particularly marked among young people with low levels of education. In the preceding United States example, those female early leavers who worked in the first year spent only 65 per cent of the next four years working, compared to 85 per cent for men. Women with only lower secondary education who did not get jobs in the first year worked only a quarter of the time over the next four years, compared to half for men.

- For those poorly-qualified youth who spend the first year after leaving school outside the labour force altogether, the proportion of time spent employed over the next four years is lower than for those who are unemployed in the first year. For example, in the case of Australia the difference amounts to an average of four percentage points less time in work for young men, and 12 percentage points less for young women.

These data reinforce the need for close monitoring of school leavers' labour market experiences and early action to ensure access to employment. Getting a job early matters, especially for those whose educational attainment is low.

Looking at the first five years out of school as a whole, there is striking variation in the experiences of people with low levels of qualifications in different countries. Figure 3.4 shows the average number of years that young people who have not completed upper secondary education are likely to spend employed over the first five years after leaving school in the five countries surveyed. This varies for men from 3.3 years in the United States to 4.4 in Germany, and for women from 1.7 years to 3.9 years in the same countries. It is also worth noting that:

- In some countries, notably Germany, being unemployed during the first year after leaving school early made less of a difference than in others to future working patterns. For example, women in Germany who were unemployed in the first year after leaving school spent on average half of the next five years working, rather than only a quarter as in the United States.

- People with higher qualifications are normally more likely to work in the years after leaving education than the less qualified. However the average of 4.4 years that young German men with low qualifications spend employed during their first five years in the labour force is actually greater than the 4.2 years spent working on average by young Australian men who have completed tertiary education (see data for Figure 3.4, p. 79). Since the young Germans concerned would not normally be qualified apprentices, these national differences among the employment experiences of education leavers are not due just to the features of the vocational training system.

Changes in skill demands

Young people are also entering labour markets in which the particular types of skills and qualifications that are in demand are changing. A shift of employment away from agriculture and industry and towards the service sector of the economy is common to most countries. Employment in many service sector industries, such as retailing, hospitality and tourism, is youth intensive. Youth

Figure 3.4
Employment after leaving school early
Average number of years spent employed over the first five years after leaving initial education by persons whose highest level of educational attainment is lower secondary education

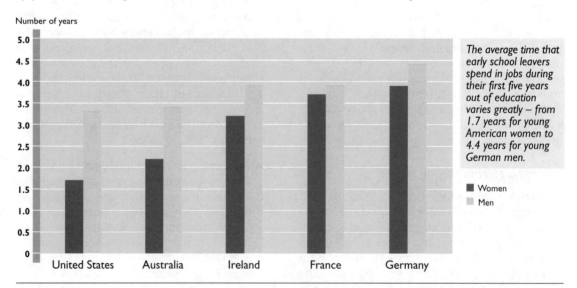

The average time that early school leavers spend in jobs during their first five years out of education varies greatly — from 1.7 years for young American women to 4.4 years for young German men.

■ Women
▨ Men

Source: OECD (1998b).
Data for Figure 3.4: page 79.

Figure 3.5
Young people in service industries
Service sector employment as a proportion of total employment, youth and adults, early 1990s

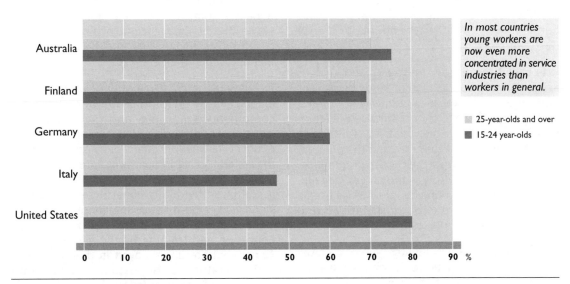

In most countries young workers are now even more concentrated in service industries than workers in general.

25-year-olds and over
15-24 year-olds

Source: OECD Education Database.
Data for Figure 3.5: page 79.

employment is highly concentrated in a small number of industries. As Figure 3.5 shows, in most countries it is also more highly concentrated in the service sector than is adult employment (see also OECD, 1996*b*).

Service industry jobs can favour young people partly for positive reasons – for example where they require computer skills, adaptability or a proficiency in foreign languages. However, there are also many low-skill jobs in sectors like retailing and tourism where young people are over-represented.

The pathways into the service sector are often less clearly delineated than those into other sectors. Vocational qualifications in these industries are often recent in origin, not widely understood by employers, and less frequently required for employment than in other industries. Employers in service industries are likely to place particular emphasis on personal qualities, experience and general competences when selecting employees. Although young people cannot readily make up for lack of experience, the extent to which they acquire general skills through education and broad life

experiences out of school can make a big difference to their prospects. So in some service industries such as finance, insurance, real estate and business services, there are few jobs for young people without some educational qualification. Conversely, poorly educated young people are over-represented in some non-service industries such as agriculture, forestry and fishing, but these generally account for very small and declining proportions of total youth employment (Freysson, 1997).

4. PATHWAYS THROUGH EDUCATION AND INTO WORK

The ways in which young people move from initial education to employment depend on a complex set of interacting conditions. The nature of the available routes through education and training and into a first job are of particular relevance to policy makers.

Education systems in different countries vary greatly in the degree to which general and vocational studies complement each other and in the ways in which they are sequenced. Countries differ, for example, in terms of whether general and vocational streams run in parallel or in integrated programmes, in terms of the breadth and depth of occupational qualifications, and in terms of the timing and nature of the choices that young people have to make between distinct pathways and labour market destinations.

It is useful to analyse the routes and choices available in terms of different kinds of *pathway*. Some are organised in *"institutionalised"* ways: young people have to choose between different programmes but have then relatively little choice over the courses that they take and the moment at which they "exit" from the chosen programme. Other pathways follow a more *"individually-constructed"* pattern: young people choose from a large range of frequently modularised and separately certified courses.

Very broadly speaking, the first type of pathway encourages the completion of programmes leading to recognised qualifications, while the latter type emphasises young people's personal initiative and responsibility in composing their own qualification profiles and determining their own exit points. Institutionalised pathways offer greater protection in the years after compulsory schooling; individually-constructed ones may offer greater flexibility to leave and later re-enter the system to build on partial qualifications. Parallel to these differences in pathways to qualification are mechanisms for entry into the labour market. In some systems this transition is dominated by collective agreements and regulations, with negotiations between employers, governments and trade unions playing an important role. Elsewhere, choices and connections between education and employment are left much more to the individual young person.

Looking more specifically at the types of pathway on offer immediately after compulsory education, most young people go through one of three routes: general education; predominantly school-based vocational pathways leading to work, to further education or to both; and apprenticeship-type pathways in which learning within paid employment is combined with classroom learning. Part A of Figure 3.6 shows how many young people take each of these options in four countries whose transition arrangements are quite different, but which typify the range of

approaches in OECD countries: Australia, Austria, the Czech Republic, and Norway. Part B of Figure 3.6 shows that these countries also have varied outcomes in terms of how many young people remain in some form of education at the age of 18 (an intermediate outcome of immediate post-compulsory provision) and how many are unemployed in their early 20s.

In *Australia* the great majority of young people enter a general education pathway at the end of compulsory schooling, and the choice of a vocational pathway is both delayed and made by relatively few people. Many of those completing the general education pathway enter work rather than further study. Transition to work thus follows a highly "individually-constructed" model. A significant minority of young people have difficulties in the transition process: 12 per cent leave education and training by the age of 16, and 10 per cent are unemployed in their early 20s. Various features of the pattern of education-employment linkages in Australia are similar to those in much of Canada, in New Zealand, and in the United States.

In *Austria* young people choose between a general education and several vocational pathways at a relatively young age. Most opt for vocational/ technical pathways: a shorter or a long school-based vocational route (the latter qualifying young people for both technician level work and higher education), or apprenticeship. Most general education graduates enter tertiary study. This highly "institutionalised" model is also very inclusive: at the age of 16 only about 3 per cent of young people are not involved in education or training, and youth unemployment is low. Similar structures are found in other German-speaking countries and in Denmark.

In the *Czech Republic*, as in Austria, the choice between a general education and several vocational pathways is made at an early age, with most choosing the latter – but in this case the vocational options are all school-based. Each vocational pathway offers several possible exit points, one of which can qualify young people for tertiary study as well as for work. Most general education graduates enter tertiary education. At the age of 15 just 2 per cent of young people are not involved in education or training. The emphasis upon school-based vocational pathways

Figure 3.6
Pathways from school into work

Structure and duration of pathways from compulsory schooling to the labour market and further education, and selected education and employment outcomes, in four countries

A. Pathways

Percentage of cohort

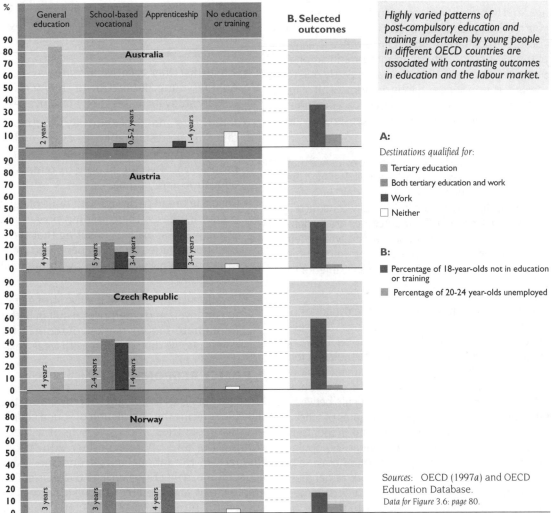

Highly varied patterns of post-compulsory education and training undertaken by young people in different OECD countries are associated with contrasting outcomes in education and the labour market.

A:

Destinations qualified for:

- Tertiary education
- Both tertiary education and work
- Work
- Neither

B:

- Percentage of 18-year-olds not in education or training
- Percentage of 20-24 year-olds unemployed

Sources: OECD (1997a) and OECD Education Database.

Data for Figure 3.6: page 80.

has points in common with approaches found in countries such as France and Italy.

In *Norway* the youth cohort is divided fairly evenly at the age of 16 between those who enter general education and those entering one of two vocational pathways. Structural linkages allow the latter to transfer to the general education pathway in order to qualify for tertiary education. Many of

those completing the general education pathway enter work rather than further study. So Norway combines institutional pathways with aspects of individual construction – apparently with some success. At the age of 16, only 3 per cent of young people are not involved in education or training, and non-participation remains low at age 18. The Norwegian approach has much in common with that found in Sweden.

The outcomes shown in Figure 3.6 are related at least in part to the nature and structure of pathways taken. In Austria, the very low proportion of 20-24 year-olds who are unemployed appears to owe much to the ability of the vocational pathways in that country to connect a high proportion of young people to the labour market at a relatively early age, and to provide another significant part of the youth cohort (about 20 per cent) with high quality vocational qualifications combined with university entry certification. The high rate of educational participation at age 18 in Norway is partly due to the later starting age and long duration of all of its pathways, but also to the diversity of programs that they offer to meet the needs and interests of a wide spectrum of young people.

More generally, there is considerable evidence that institutional pathways can, where well designed, be effective in steering most young people into employment. The evidence on individually-constructed pathways is less clear. Their outcomes are by definition harder to pinpoint and classify, while their overall performance in terms of employment rates have been mixed rather than universally inferior to more institutionalised systems.

However, looking more closely at the dynamics of the transition, it appears that countries with well-developed pathways from education to work succeed in getting young people into their first job quickly, and in limiting long-term youth unemployment. This is important given the evidence discussed above showing the relationship between initial and subsequent employment rates of school leavers. Figure 3.7 shows that in general, in countries with the lowest youth unemployment to population ratios, the unemployed are often making a relatively short-term transition to work, rather than being long-term unemployed. In the three countries with youth unemployment rates of 10 per cent or below in 1995 – Austria, Denmark and Germany – relatively small minorities of the young unemployed were looking for their first job or had been out of work for over a year. These are all countries with well-defined institutionalised pathways, with strong links into employment. In contrast, in three of the five countries with the highest youth unemployment – Finland, Greece and Italy – three-quarters of those seeking jobs were looking for their first one, and in Greece and Italy at least half had been looking for work for over a year.

Analysis of pathways, and of their relationship to education and labour market outcomes (OECD, 1996*b* and 1998*a*) suggests the following lessons:

- Delaying entry to vocational pathways can reduce their attractiveness to young people, especially in countries where choices have traditionally had to be made at an early age, or where the value of vocational qualifications in the labour market is perceived to be unsatisfactory.

- Ensuring that vocational pathways can qualify young people for both work and tertiary study increases their attractiveness.

- Offering a range of pathways suited to differing interests and needs at the end of compulsory education encourages a higher proportion of young people to remain in education and training.

- Ensuring broad pathways with multiple exit points increases their holding power and attractiveness, as does ensuring that there are opportunities for young people to cross from one pathway to another with minimal loss of time.

- Vocational pathways that involve strong links to employers and enterprises result in better immediate labour market outcomes for young people than do those with weak links.

5. POLICY RESPONSES

The above analysis has demonstrated some of the difficulties facing the one-quarter of young people in OECD countries who leave school without completing an upper-secondary education. Changes in the labour market and the wider economy mean that they find it hard to gain stable employment and thereby to start a process of successful integration into society. Without recognised qualifications, they are more likely to enter part-time or temporary work, or unemployment, or be outside the labour force altogether. Longitudinal analyses suggest that a poor start in the labour market can be difficult to overcome, especially for those with low levels of initial qualifications.

A strategy to ensure that young people are equipped for an effective transition to work and adult life should therefore aim first and foremost to prevent

Figure 3.7
Characteristics of the young unemployed, 1995
Percentage of 15-24 year-olds who are unemployed, who are seeking their first job, or who have been unemployed for 12 months or more

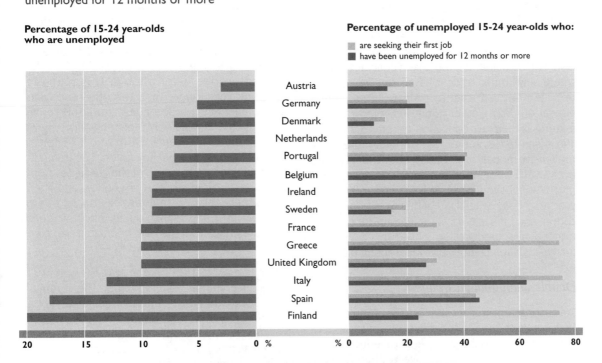

Percentage of 15-24 year-olds who are unemployed

Percentage of unemployed 15-24 year-olds who:
- are seeking their first job
- have been unemployed for 12 months or more

In countries where many young people are unemployed, they are often more likely than average to have moved directly from education to unemployment or to have been out of work for over a year.

Source: EUROSTAT (1997).
Data for Figure 3.7: page 80.

failure at school. However, improving success in education is not, on its own, sufficient for overcoming youth unemployment and other problems in the transition to work and adult society. The evidence shows that both for groups with and without educational qualifications, early labour market prospects vary greatly from one country to another.

Apprenticeship systems in the German-speaking and some other countries have a good track record of keeping youth unemployment in the 15-19 age group at comparatively very low levels and at ensuring that these labour market benefits persist for young adults. This has led to many efforts at developing similar arrangements in other countries. Over the years it has become obvious, however, that a whole range of social, economic and political conditions need to be fulfilled for apprenticeship

systems to function successfully. Such conditions include the self-organisation of employers and their collective co-operation with public authorities in designing and implementing training regulations, as well as the content and modes of certification. Another necessary condition seems to be the existence of a strong sense of social partnership between governments, employers and trade unions, which obliges those involved in designing and regulating apprenticeship systems to collaborate and negotiate. This means that responses to changing needs and conditions can only be implemented after lengthy and extensive analysis, consultation and policy debate among all the actors who then tend to identify with, and support, the negotiated outcomes. Substantial resources, including patience, are required for these processes to work their way through.

These conditions are far from being fulfilled in most OECD countries. Moreover, the apprenticeship countries typically have education systems where lower secondary education is non-comprehensive (that is, children are tracked into at least two different streams at a young age), where general and vocational pathways are often strongly isolated from each other at the upper secondary level, and where only limited bridges have been established between apprenticeship training and higher education. Many other countries rejected such features of their own education systems during the 1960s and 1970s, and moved towards more comprehensive models of secondary education. Finally, even in the apprenticeship countries, increasing proportions of young people have tended in recent years to choose general rather than vocational education, and full-time vocational/technical schools rather than apprenticeship, while firms have been increasingly reluctant to provide training places.

Double-qualifying pathways

Traditional apprenticeship arrangements may therefore not provide the most relevant "model" for other OECD countries seeking to reduce youth unemployment and to improve young people's transition from education to work. More broadly applicable solutions in the long run may lie in developing pathways that respond flexibly to young people's desire to access tertiary education, and at the same time provide them with occupational qualifications that are valued in the labour market. Depending on the occupational structures and the readiness of enterprises to provide training in each industry, such pathways may encompass many types of early contact with the labour market, ranging from formal apprenticeships to internships and student projects.

A number of countries, especially in Europe, are currently seeking to develop double-qualifying pathways that can lead to both tertiary education and the labour market. Pathways that provide such combinations of qualifications can encourage lifelong learning, by enabling students to see the worlds of work and study as intertwined. The effective provision of such pathways, though, requires far-reaching changes in curriculum, pedagogy and assessment, and strong partnerships between schools, enterprises and tertiary institutions.

Austria is a particularly interesting country in this respect, because it has for many years offered a vocational/technical pathway in full-time schools (BHS) that is highly regarded by employers and which also provides access to higher education. The curriculum of these schools usually includes obligatory summer internships, in which students are typically required to solve real problems in the host enterprise. Even though this pathway takes one year longer than the other four-year programmes of upper secondary education, young Austrians are increasingly preferring this type of programme to apprenticeship and to shorter school-based vocational education. The immediate employment prospects of the graduates from the BHS schools are at least as good as, and often better then, those of apprentices. In addition, because of the access their qualification provides to higher education, the BHS graduates are often able to build more substantial careers.

Other types of institution that have the potential to produce similar results include the community colleges of North America. While serving a much more varied population, they offer school leavers the opportunity to obtain occupational qualifications and/or to prepare for entry into higher education. Although the community colleges may not have the structured forms of enterprise involvement and workplace contact of the Austrian-type institutions, many have developed successful partnerships with local and regional industry, as well as with higher education institutions.

Policy coherence

Beyond consideration of the specific organisational forms that post-compulsory education and training pathways should take, there is the wider issue of how societies can develop coherent education, labour and social policies to help young people in their transition to work and adult life. The most sustained example of such coherence is probably to be found in the *youth guarantee* approach which the Nordic countries have been developing over the past two decades. The evolution of this idea has led to the concept of a guaranteed *opportunity* for all through a position in either education, training or work. Whether each individual takes up the opportunity is ultimately his or her own decision. However, a system of incentives and penalties, and tight safety nets for those who fail, helps young people to develop towards useful and productive roles.

The Nordic experience has gradually shown that a policy distinction needs to be made between those below and above the age range of upper secondary education. While the most appropriate response to at-risk teenagers lies in keeping them in school (or apprenticeship) or reintegrating them in education or training as rapidly as possible, the measures required for 20-24 year-olds need to be different in kind. Such measures need to concentrate on entry into stable employment, in conjunction with strategies to improve skills training. This can take the form, for example, of raising age limits for apprenticeship and various educational programmes where such barriers exist, and of giving subsidies or tax relief to employers who provide work associated with training. For this group of young adults it is also essential that the balance of incentives and penalties in unemployment and welfare support encourages them to take up employment and training measures.

Youth unemployment has not been eradicated in the Nordic countries. However, the number of very young people in the labour market has been considerably reduced, and much stronger partnerships have been developed between educational institutions and enterprises. The Norwegian and Swedish experiences in particular show the value of individualised follow-up measures for those who have left school early, or who are at risk of leaving early. Such services, in which municipal governments play key roles, can be resource intensive. However, the Nordic experience also shows that there is no inevitability about the number of early school leavers, and that chances for successful intervention seem to be higher while young people are still in school. Intensive measures to help early leavers in the labour market can be all the more effective if resources are freed up by keeping their numbers low in the first place.

6. CONCLUSIONS

Although their institutional frameworks and pathways differ, the approaches in both the Nordic and the traditional apprenticeship countries have much in common. Both are based on society assuming a degree of responsibility for young people's transition from education to work, on the active engagement of employers and trade unions in policy making, programme design and certification, and on focused efforts to ensure that young people do not "fall through the cracks" after leaving initial education and training. Both approaches also make social, economic and educational aspects of youth policy complementary and mutually reinforcing. Such broad policy principles, if not specific structures distinctive to each country's traditions and institutions, are transferable to youth policy across a wide range of countries. ■

References

EUROSTAT (1997), *Youth in the European Union. From Education to Working Life*, European Communities, Luxembourg.

FREYSSON, L. (1997), "Labour market exclusion of young people: Some illustrations of the situation in the European Union", Paper presented to the European Workshop on Transitions in Youth, Dublin.

OECD (1996*a*), "Transition from school to work", *Education at a Glance – Analysis*, Paris.

OECD (1996*b*), "Growing into work", *Employment Outlook*, Paris.

OECD (1997*a*), *Education at a Glance – OECD Indicators 1997*, Paris.

OECD (1997*b*), *Labour Market Policies: New Challenges. Lifelong Learning to Maintain Employability*, OECD/GD(97)162, Paris.

OECD (1997*c*), *Post-compulsory Education for Disabled People*, Paris.

OECD (1998*a*), *Pathways and Participation in Vocational Education and Training*, Paris.

OECD (1998*b*), "Getting started, settling in: The transition from education to the labour market", *Employment Outlook 1998*, Paris.

CHAPTER 4

PAYING FOR TERTIARY EDUCATION:
The learner perspective

SUMMARY

While tertiary education continues to be considered a largely public enterprise, students and their families are making substantial contributions both to the cost of tuition and to other expenses associated with study, in a number of countries. The share of expenditures of tertiary education institutions covered by students and their families now ranges widely, from a negligible amount in Denmark, Sweden and Austria to almost 40 per cent in the United States, and over half in Korea and Japan. The share of spending has been increasing in different ways in different countries, such as new imposition of fees, reductions in subsidies to goods and services bought by students, and a greater rate of enrolment expansion in private than in public institutions.

But the private cost of tertiary education also varies widely for different students and their families within individual countries. Those who enrol part-time, who enrol in certain courses or institutions, who enrol in private institutions, who are above a certain age or who fail to exceed a certain level of academic achievement even though they qualify for courses, can all end up bearing higher costs. Countries need to consider whether existing financing policies push students down certain tracks rather than enabling them to follow pathways that meet their needs. A "level playing field" of finance is a more useful starting-point than the structures that exist for historical reasons.

What effect do private costs have on student choices? While it is difficult to disentangle the many influences on student behaviour, expansion in some countries has not seen an increase in the representation of low income families. It should be emphasised that evidence of the links between private payments and behaviour remains limited and uneven.

Nonetheless, both the allocation of costs to different students and their families and how those costs, once allocated, are to be financed have to be looked at carefully to maximise the degree to which all aspiring students can take choices about a wide range of study options and routes.

1. INTRODUCTION

During the 1990s, increasingly varied forms of tertiary education have become available to a growing number of students. These trends of growing participation and diversification have not simply been driven by "supply-side" decisions by governments to fund places. A major driving force has been demand – the choices made by learners (see OECD, 1997*a* and 1998). Decisions by young people and adults to participate in tertiary education have always been influenced partly by economic considerations – notably the trade-off between earnings forgone while studying and the greater prospective future earnings that result. Recently, the economic component in private decisions about participation has grown in the many countries where individuals are having to contribute more than in the past to the cost of tuition and living expenses.

So analysis of the financing of tertiary education needs to move beyond the question of how many places are provided by governments and institutions. It should also look at the contribution made by students and their families, at the incentives that exist for them to invest in tertiary education, and at how they respond to these incentives. Such an analysis needs to identify the different costs actually incurred by different learners according to what, when, how and where they study. An understanding of student costs and incentives seems essential if countries are to adopt a more strategic approach to tertiary education policies, reflecting a new view of the student – in the words of Australia's West Committee, as a "sophisticated client" rather than a "passive consumer" (DEETYA, 1998).

This chapter considers evidence on three aspects of individual decisions to invest in tertiary education. First, it charts the degree to which the visible costs of tertiary education are being borne more than in the past by students and their families. Second, it analyses the patterns of how these costs fall, pointing to important variations according to the situation of each student, which can be difficult to justify if students are to have equal chances under highly diverse circumstances. Third, the chapter looks at the impact of private financing on participation and overall spending levels, finding a complex picture that does not show clear effects of the imposition of costs on students and households.

Figure. 4.1 **The costs of tertiary education**

Visible costs	Invisible costs
Direct cost of education provided Covered by payments to educational institutions, mainly via: – Block grants from governments – Student fees funded by governments – Fees paid by students from own means	**Forgone earnings**
Other expenses associated with studying *e.g.:* – Equipment and books – Living expenses – Transport	

2. PRIVATE SPENDING ON THE "VISIBLE" COSTS OF TERTIARY EDUCATION

Tertiary education is still considered a mainly public enterprise, yet involves a substantial and growing degree of private financing for its "visible" costs. These costs (see Box 4.1) include both the cost of tuition and other spending that needs to be incurred in order to study.

The amount incurred by students for fees and other education-related expenses differs among countries according to taxation and spending policies and to the willingness of governments to support students, influenced by whether they are studying full- or part-time, and whether they are living in their families' homes. To some extent the patterns of attendance that have helped determine these subsidy patterns are breaking down. More mature students, whose numbers are increasing, are more likely to have established their own households and to prefer part-time and distance learning to full-time, on campus study. New forms of study often incorporate periods of work. Increasing numbers of students of all ages work while following studies. In some cases the siting of new institutions in underserved areas or a toughening of restrictions on entry to local institutions have affected the proportions studying while living at home.

BOX 4.1 WHAT IS MEANT BY "VISIBLE" COSTS OF TERTIARY EDUCATION?

This chapter focuses on the "visible" cost to learners of participating in tertiary education. These are defined as all those things that must be paid for in order to study. They include direct payments to institutions for tuition as well as other fees for application, examination or registration. Other costs of study, not paid to institutions, include the purchase of books, equipment and supplies. Visible costs also include important types of spending that are needed to make study possible even though they are not on academic items: notably on lodgings, meals and transportation.

As portrayed in Figure 4.1, it is not only students who bear the direct cost of providing tertiary education – indeed, in most European countries it has traditionally been financed almost entirely by block grants from governments to institutions. The alternative is for institutions to receive fees for each student, although students do not always bear all, or any, of the cost. One option is simply to pay government grants to institutions, but on a per-student rather than block grant basis. Another is to repay to students some of the tuition fees that they incur, through grants, tax breaks or subsidised loans. Employers also sometimes help with tuition costs. This chapter is concerned principally with the *net* cost that falls on the student or household. The same applies to indirect costs such as board and lodging, which may also be partly defrayed by government through grants or subsidies to services.

The "invisible" cost of time devoted to studies by learners is not included in this analysis. This consists of earnings forgone for the duration of the study period. Insofar as some earnings would need to be used for living expenses had the student not enrolled, this part of earnings forgone should not be counted as fully additional to the visible costs including room and board. Earnings forgone represent a significant share of the costs borne by learners, and these enter into decisions of individuals about whether to participate in tertiary education as well as the choice of study option (*e.g.*, part-time study while employed as opposed to full-time study without earnings from employment).

The perspective of costs differs for tertiary institutions and for public authorities. The former look at the programmes and teaching through which learning is organised and supported and how these are financed, while the latter are concerned with all resources required to permit learning, encompassing instruction and living costs, forgone earnings and incentives and barriers to participation of learners.

Public funds to help students and their families meet tertiary education costs are provided in a variety of ways, including grants, student loans, allowances and tax breaks. While repayment of loans or deferred payment of contributions or charges are made from the graduate's income, in most such schemes governments help reduce the private costs. They do so through mechanisms such as guaranting the principal, imposing below-market interest rates, paying interest while the student is enrolled or on behalf of the graduate in periods of low earnings. They may also forgive debt or payment obligation if borrowers enter particular fields or occupations, die before the obligation is paid or experience low earnings over a lifetime. By some estimates, these features lead to implicit subsidies ranging from 10 to 50 per cent or more of the loan amount, with the balance constituting private or household spending on tertiary education.

Some countries concentrate support to students rather on allowances and subsidies that make meals, housing and other services cheaper; in the Czech Republic and France, such measures are estimated to amount to over 0.2 per cent of GDP. In the French case, it is estimated that these subsidies to students are almost one-fifth as great as direct spending on tertiary institutions. Such subsidies do not favour all students evenly: those who study full-time and who are dependent on their parents gain most, which raises issues of targeting.

Comparative data on spending by students and their families on tertiary education are limited. Available data for a number of countries permit comparisons of private payments for tertiary education to institutions and household payments as a separate component of private

Figure 4.2
The private contribution to tertiary education
Spending on educational institutions, by source

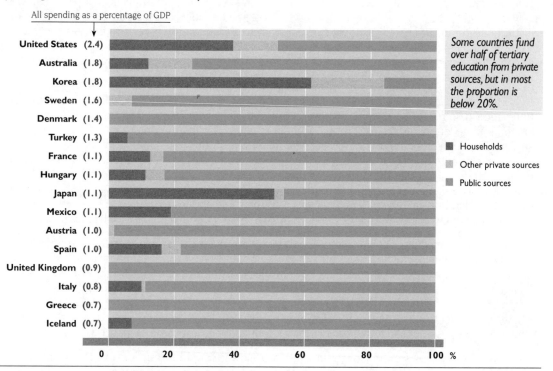

All spending as a percentage of GDP

United States (2.4)
Australia (1.8)
Korea (1.8)
Sweden (1.6)
Denmark (1.4)
Turkey (1.3)
France (1.1)
Hungary (1.1)
Japan (1.1)
Mexico (1.1)
Austria (1.0)
Spain (1.0)
United Kingdom (0.9)
Italy (0.8)
Greece (0.7)
Iceland (0.7)

0   20   40   60   80   100 %

Some countries fund over half of tertiary education from private sources, but in most the proportion is below 20%.

■ Households
▨ Other private sources
■ Public sources

Source: OECD Education Database.
Data for Figure 4.2: page 81.

payments.[1] As shown in Figure 4.2, the share of educational expenditures of tertiary institutions covered by individuals, businesses and other private sources together, *net* of public financial aid to students and subsidies to other private entities, ranges widely in OECD countries, from a negligible amount in Denmark, Greece and the United Kingdom to over half in the United States, Korea and Japan, with five other countries (Australia, France, Hungary, Mexico and Spain) obtaining 15-25 per cent of funding from private sources.[2] Figure 4.2 also puts the total tertiary education spending on institutions in context, by expressing it as a percentage of GDP. It is worth noting that some of the countries with the highest total spending relative to national income, such as the United States, Australia and Korea, muster these resources with substantial help from private means. Conversely, in several countries with relatively low overall spending such as Austria, the United Kingdom and Greece, private sources tend to contribute relatively little.

But these tendencies are not rigid rules: Australia for example spends two-thirds more as a share of its GDP on tertiary education than Japan, but only 25 per cent of this spending in Australia compared to 54 per cent in Japan comes from private sources.

Household[3] payments to tertiary education institutions, *net* of money refunded for example in government grants to defray tuition costs, also vary widely as a source of funds for tertiary educational expenditure. The net household share of expenditure averages about 12.9 per cent for the sixteen countries with comparable coverage in the data. As shown in Figure 4.2, households in Korea and Japan cover much more of the costs in their countries (62 per cent and 51 per cent, respectively) than do their counterparts in most European countries. In Europe, spending by students and their families accounts for less than 20 per cent of expenditures on tertiary education institutions, with the shares greater than 10 per cent in Spain, France, Hungary and Italy.

Figure 4.3
Growth in funding for tertiary education by source in the early 1990s
Average annual percentage increase

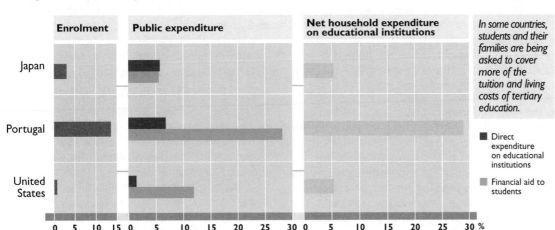

Source: OECD Secretariat, based on country-provided information for thematic review of the first years of tertiary education.
Data for Figure 4.3: page 81.

A notable trend is that the net amount contributed by households to tertiary education expenditures increased in several OECD countries in the first half of the 1990s. As shown in Figure 4.3, net household spending increased by an average annual rate of 5 to about 30 per cent in three countries for which trend data are available. The data refer to household spending on tuition costs *net* of financial aid to students to cover those costs.

Individual data on countries show that in those countries where household spending on tuition fees, education-related services and living costs is increasing, the growth is due to one or more of four factors.

a. Enrolments have increased, as in Australia, France and Portugal, contributing to increases in the volume of spending on tertiary education by households in those countries. While enrolments have also grown in such countries as Finland, the impact is less owing to nearly full public support for tuition and living costs. Nevertheless, Finnish students may finance their living costs with a bank loan guaranteed by the government which obliges repayment, and younger students commonly receive at least some additional support from their parents.

b. Fees, charges or contributions have been increased or newly imposed in a wide range of

1. The available data do not cover expenditure on other tertiary-level options. Coverage of other "visible" costs of other education-related and living expenses is uneven and incomplete. Moreover, the attribution of expenses by source, including households, is problematic. Third-party transfers to learners or their families, *e.g.* from employers, are not recorded in most system or institutional accounts and tax breaks are unevenly reported. Some of these shortcomings can be addressed through well-designed surveys of prospective and current students and their families which draw on financial records and the use of diaries; such surveys have been carried out in some countries. Another approach is to develop "notional" profiles of costs and sources of financing (*e.g.*, Johnstone, 1985 and Table 4.1 below). These provide benchmarks against which countries can be compared, but fail to take into account more diverse pathways and combinations of studies. A more significant problem is definition. There is no agreed means to account for the public subsidy and private shares of student loan or deferred payment schemes or tax breaks. Uneven coverage arising from the inability to address these definition and measurement issues is likely to become a more significant problem as diverse patterns of participation become the norm and the use of student loans, tax credits and other alternative financing schemes increases.

2. Private expenditure on tertiary education institutions includes grants and contracts including those negotiated with employers for customised teaching, endowment income and alumni giving. Borrowing from private banks, even if guaranteed and partly subsidised by governments, are reported by some countries in the OECD Education Database as private expenditures other than by households. It is *net* of public financial aid to students and public subsidies to other private entities, but does not exclude the value of tax breaks provided for educational expenses.

3. "Household" refers to individual students and their families.

countries. This applies in Portugal, the United States and Japan, but also to Australia, the Netherlands, Italy, the United Kingdom and New Zealand. Some governments draw on fees to cover a greater proportion of the costs of large volume participation in tertiary education, so the growth in subsidies to students helped households meet only a share of the increased costs in those countries.

c. The cost of education-related goods and services other than instruction has risen, or subsidies for them per student are lower. Information on education-related and living expenses are uneven, but country-provided data indicate increases on such expenditure over the 1990 to 1994 period of about 7 per cent in Japan and 5 per cent in the United States. The Netherlands has reduced the subsidy to cover these expenses, as have the United Kingdom, Finland, Germany, and New Zealand. The shift has resulted partly from a relative increase in the volume of student loans that, even taking into account features which reduce the costs to students of loan origination and repayment, require students or their families to assume a larger share of tertiary education costs. In Germany, for example, those eligible for financial aid receive equal parts grant and loan; in Sweden and Norway, the loan component accounts for 70 per cent of the support provided to financial aid recipients.

d. A higher percentage of enrolment in some countries is in independent private institutions[4] with higher fees that have to cover nearly the full cost of tuition: this is the case in Portugal, Japan, Korea and the United States among other countries. In Portugal, virtually all spending by students and families on tertiary education institutions in 1995-96 went to private universities and polytechnics. Those institutions accounted for about one-third of overall enrolment, up from about 20 per cent in 1990.

It is important to recognise that rises in tuition fees, in private institution enrolments and in educational costs generally do not necessarily imply that increased private spending has been accompanied by falls in public expenditures on tertiary education. As shown in Figure 4.3, in Japan and the United States, public spending on tertiary education institutions has increased despite rising tuition fees, partly because enrolment continues to grow,

the share of enrolment in public institutions has been maintained and financial aid to students has grown. There also remain countries that have financed expansion mainly out of public budgets, and where private spending for tertiary education remains negligible. One such country is Finland, as already noted; others are Denmark, Sweden, Belgium (Flanders) and Germany.

In countries with means-tested financial aid or tuition fees, parents are expected to cover part of the net private cost of their children's participation in tertiary education. In these and other countries, parent or family support is provided for younger students in a variety of ways, as is support provided by the families of mature age students. Less visible intra-family transfers, such as housing for the student family member or cash gifts from grandparents, can be difficult to quantify. It is clear however that they are significant in value. Drawing on information collected in a 1994 survey carried out by the *Observatoire de la vie étudiante*, Eicher and Gruel (1996) estimate that somewhat more than 40 per cent of the resources for students are provided by parents in the forms of direct cash support, payments on behalf of students or in-kind support for lodging and meals. While the amounts provided by parents are less for students who are older and live away from home, they account on average for over one-fifth of the resources available to students in this group.[5] According to survey data in the United States, grandparents and other relatives provide as much as 10 per cent of "out-of-pocket" costs for low income students.

Some of the costs falling on students and families can be recouped through tax breaks, which reduce tax liabilities to reflect parent and family contributions to educational costs. Information on the value of tax breaks is not readily available on a comparative basis. For the United States, tax

---

4. The terms "independent private" and "private" are used interchangeably in this chapter to refer to institutions which receive most of their core funding from non-government sources.

5. The estimates refer, respectively, to all students and to students from a middle class background (parents who are shopkeepers, crafts workers, heads of firms and mid-level professionals), aged 24 or older and who live away from home. See Eicher and Gruel (1996), Tables 2.13, 2.26, 2.27 and p. 85.

expenditures account for about 3 per cent of the costs of tertiary education, a proportion that is expected to increase sharply with recently-enacted legislation providing for an additional $7 billion per year in tax reductions for students and their families. To place this sum in perspective, about $50 billion in financial aid was awarded to tertiary education students in 1995-96.

So the pattern of private spending on tertiary education is complex. It is increasing in magnitude and scope in many countries, but it does not obviously displace public spending or even necessarily take a growing share of an expanding level of provision. There are also ways in which public support can play new or expanded roles, for example through the increase in tax breaks. The one generalisation that can be made is that private means are increasingly being brought into an evolving *partnership* to cover the cost of educating a widening section of the population at tertiary level.

3. **WHO PAYS WHAT?**

The proportion of spending on tertiary education that falls to students and their families is far from evenly spread within each country. The split between public subsidy and private contribution differs significantly according to various study options or student characteristics including time spent studying, type or field of course, control of institution, age and academic achievement, among others. Such differences are important for the (dis)incentives that they create to study. The broad approach to lifelong learning described in Chapter 1 above would in general argue against financing arrangements which have the effect of channeling students into specific and rigid routes at particular ages, rather than permitting learners to make choices among programmes according to whether they meet individual needs. This does not mean that costs should be exactly equal for every student, but that the reasons for difference and the effect of different incentives should be carefully considered. This becomes all the more important in the light of new, innovative approaches to the financing of household spending for tertiary education. Brief descriptions of some of those approaches are provided in Box 4.2 (page 67).

Table 4.1 (page 64) shows how public support and private contributions differ according to the attributes of students and the study options they choose. Costs can vary according to:

Part- or full-time study

Part-time learners face higher costs than full-time students in a number of countries. In Sweden and the United States only those enrolled half-time or more are eligible for such support. In Denmark and the Netherlands, students following courses in Open Education or Open Universities, usually on a part-time basis, pay tuition fees which generally are greater than those paid by full-time students (full-time students in Danish tertiary education pay no tuition fees). In the Dutch and Danish cases, fees in open learning programmes are set at the discretion of the providing institution. Part-time attendance is recognised in Australia, where students enrolled less than full-time assume a Higher Education Contribution proportional to their course load. Part-time students are not eligible for support through the Youth Allowance. In most OECD countries, employers cover all or part of fees for employees following courses part-time.[6] In a number of European countries, there is no clear distinction between full- and part-time study. However, in some of these countries, students who do not complete "on time" most or all of the first one or two years of a student programme may lose eligibility for grants or for low or no tuition fees.

Whether university course

In some countries university students are treated more favourably than others. In Japan, most special training colleges charge nearly full-cost fees; the same is true for career schools (but not community colleges) in the United States. In both countries, students following courses at these types of tertiary education institutions are eligible for student financial aid to cover all costs. Advanced vocational studies in TAFE Institutes in Australia attract higher levels of public support relative to educational costs; learners in these programmes are eligible for financial aid.

---

6. Funding arrangements are highly variable, within and among countries. This is, in part, because the distinction between regular study programmes and continuing professional education or customised training modules is increasingly blurred. See OECD (1995).

Table 4.1
Variables associated with differences in costs to tertiary education students and their families, selected countries

	AUSTRALIA	AUSTRIA	DENMARK	FINLAND	FRANCE	GERMANY
Part- or full-time studies	Part-time students have access to HECS, but no Youth Allowance support.		Fees for part-time students in Open Education vary by programme, as decided by each institution.			
Whether university	Students in other tertiary education courses pay lower fees and have access to Youth Allowance.					
Field of study	Higher HECS charges for students enrolled in high cost, high demand and popular fields; Income contingent payment of HECS, favouring arts and sciences courses.			Loan with mortgage-type repayment, favouring professional programmes.		Half of support is loan with mortgage-type repayment, favouring professional programmes.
Public or private institution	Students in private institutions pay higher fees, and have no access to HECS; students attending private institutions have access to Youth Allowance provided that the institution is accredited.					
Age	Means-test includes parents' resources to age 24.	Support provided to parents of students to age 26; student support to age 39.	No age limit; more support is provided if student is more than 29 years old or living away from home; social welfare beneficiaries retain benefits for two years of study.	More support is provided if student is more than 20 years old or living away from home; targetted programme of means-tested support for students aged 25-64.	Support to age 26.	Support to age 30.
Academic achievement*		Limited number of merit awards; no support for change in orien-tation after 2 years; time-limited support (loss of support if student is more than one-year behind in the study programme).	Time-limited support, corresponding to the prescribed duration of the study programme plus 12 months.	Time-limited support (55 months for 1st degree).	Time-limited support (6 years for DEUG).	Limited number of merit awards.

	JAPAN	NETHERLANDS	NEW ZEALAND	NORWAY	SWEDEN	UNITED STATES
Part- or full-time studies		Fees for part-time study set at discretion of institution and at Open University (Open University provides support to one-third of students).			Support for students enrolled half-time or more.	Support for students enrolled half-time or more.
Whether university	Students in special training colleges pay fees; about 1% of these students receive support to cover the fees and living costs.					Support for fees and living costs is available to all tertiary education students in eligible programmes.
Field of study	Loan with mortgage-type repayment favouring professional fields; graduates in some fields exempted from repayment.	Loan with income contingent repayment, favouring arts and sciences courses.	Loan with income contingent repayment, favouring arts and sciences courses.		70% of support is loan with income contingent repayment, favouring arts and sciences courses.	Loan with mortgage-type repayment, favouring professional fields; graduates in some fields exempted from repayment.
Public or private institution	Students in private institutions pay fees (75% greater than public); about 10% of undergraduate students in private 4-year institutions receive public support for fees and living costs.	Students in public and approved private institutions are eligible for support.	Students in public and private institutions are eligible for support.	Students in public institutions and recognised programmes in private institutions are eligible for support.		Students in public and private institutions are eligible for support.
Age		Support to age 27.	Means test includes parents' income to age 24.	Support to age 65; social welfare beneficiaries retain benefits, but receive reduced support.	Support to age 45.	Means test includes parents' resources to age 24; welfare beneficiaries generally do not retain benefits.
Academic achievement*	Highest academic achievers admitted to highly competitive public institutions, where fees are lower.	Fees can increase after 6 years; time-limited support (grant eligibility is maintained if 50% of study points completed in every year; loan converted to grant if degree is completed in 6 years).		Time-limited support (5 years, 8 years for long degree programmes).	Time-limited support (6 years).	Limited number of merit awards; support contingent on "satisfactory progress".

* Includes both direct favouring of academic achievers and time-limit to funding that create higher costs to slower completers.
Source: OECD Secretariat, based on country-provided data for thematic review of the first years of tertiary education and supplementary materials.

Field of study

Students undertaking courses in the sciences or certain professional programmes may face costs or incentives which favour those fields over others. In some countries, higher tuition fees for courses in the sciences, engineering and medicine have been established to take into account the higher costs of instruction in those fields. This is the policy now in place, on a system level, in Australia where a differentiated Higher Education Contribution is assessed at one of three levels according to the cost, demand and earnings potential associated with the units of study in which a student enrols. In New Zealand and the United States, differential fees are imposed by a limited number of institutions, but in most countries such distinctions are not made. (Further details on the Australian and New Zealand experiences can be found in Box 4.2.) The cases of Japan and Portugal are different: sciences, medical and engineering programmes are offered mostly in public institutions as part of a full range of courses, while private institutional providers mostly offer programmes embracing the arts, social sciences and professions (other than health fields). A student choosing to enrol in the latter fields will, on average, incur higher tuition fees.

Complementary to differential tuition fees are targeted financial aid and the forms of financial support provided to students. Grants may be targeted on students in some fields, including the sciences; forgiveness of accumulated student loan debt may be offered as an incentive to graduates of those fields, on condition that they take up employment in particular posts or locations. This applies in Japan and the United States, but there is experience with the approach in other countries. More generally, the conditions governing repayment of student loans or contributions can affect the relative attractiveness of studies in different fields. Mortgage-type student loans found in Finland, Japan and the United States impose a schedule of defined payments over a fixed term. These conditions tend to favour enrolment in fields leading to good employment options, high and steady earnings prospects and greater scope for job mobility, such as professional studies in law, business and health-related fields. Income-contingent arrangements in which repayments or deferred payments increase with income, or are reduced during periods when income is below a minimum threshold, lower the disincentive to enrol in fields with low, less certain or less stable employment and earnings prospects such as the arts and sciences. Income-contingent schemes are found in Australia, the Netherlands, New Zealand and Sweden.

Public or private institution

As referred to above, the highest fees tend to be faced by students studying at independent private institutions. This effect is mitigated in some countries such as Japan by access to grants and loans, and in the United States, financial aid related to student means and the costs that they face create greater balance. In several European countries, including the Netherlands and Norway, students enrolled in private institutions are eligible for financial aid if they are following an approved or recognised course. Countries that regard private institutions as providing an important part of tertiary education opportunities may ask whether there should be any discrimination at all between the level of subsidy going to public and private institutions, or at least whether there is a case for aiming for a more balanced cost for students, so that they may choose among institutions on non-financial grounds. New tertiary education finance policies adopted in Portugal seek to establish just such a balance: financial support for students attending private universities and polytechnics will be increased more rapidly than funding made available to students enrolled in public sector institutions, eventually leading to student funding which narrows the differences between public and private institutions in terms of the *net* costs faced by students and their families.

Age

In some countries, governments have policies that provide more favourable support to those who have just left school than to older groups. The age at which eligibility for student support terminates is 26 in France, 27 in the Netherlands, 30 in Germany, 39 in Austria, 45 in Sweden and 65 in Norway. Finland has a targeted programme of means-tested support for adults aged 25-64; the means testing directs financial aid to those who are unemployed or otherwise lack resources to support education-related and living costs

BOX 4.2 WHO PAYS WHAT: EXAMPLES OF NEW FINANCING APPROACHES

Differentiated student contributions by field, in Australia are based on three criteria: differences in underlying costs, the earnings potential of graduates from the field and the popularity of the course. Courses are assigned to one of three bands for the differentiated Higher Education Contribution (HEC): Band 1, A$3 300, Band 2, A$4 700 and Band 3, A$5 500. On the basis of estimated cost profiles, course in arts, humanities and the social sciences are assigned to Band 1; computing, sciences and engineering to Band 2; and medicine, dentistry and veterinary science to Band 3. Taking into account criteria of earnings potential and student demand, units of study in some higher cost courses such as nursing and visual and performing arts are placed in Band 1 while units of study in some lower cost fields such as business and economics are placed in Band 2 and law is placed in Band 3.

Institution-established tuition fees, in New Zealand to cover the implicit gap between state-provided support to the public institution and anticipated costs. Large institutions charge a flat fee for all programmes; the majority differentiate fees according to the underlying cost of the course or the level of tuition subsidy which under the "study right" policy can differ by age and prior enrolment status of the student as well as the course.

Means-tested tuition fees, in the United Kingdom. From 1998-99, new full-time undergraduates will be required to contribute up to £ 1000 towards annual tuition fees. The state will meet the balance of tuition costs and cover proportionately more of those costs for students from lower income families.

Time-limited student financial aid :
– converted from loan to grant if student completes 50 per cent of study points in every year and all study points toward a degree in 6 years, as of 1998-99 in the Netherlands;
– up to 55 months for living costs while undertaking a course leading to a first degree, in Finland.

Income-contingent student loan repayment or deferred payment of student contribution in Australia, the Netherlands, New Zealand, Sweden and the United Kingdom. In the New Zealand programme, students may take out loans to cover tuition fees, course-related costs and living costs, up to a fixed maximum for each component. The interest rate is set each year, based on 10-year bond rates plus a 0.9 per cent risk premium. Repayment is proportional to the borrower's income at a rate of 10 cents on every dollar of income above a threshold (set at NZ$ 14 300 in 1996-97); when a borrower has low or no income in a given year, the interest due for that year is written off. Loan balances are adjusted to ensure that their value remains constant in real terms.

Tax breaks for tertiary education spending, in the United States which allow a credit for expenses against taxes owed or deductions to reduce income subject to taxation. From 1998, a non-refundable tax credit can be claimed of up to US$1 500 of the first US$ 2 000 of out-of-pocket tuition fees per person in each of the first two years of tertiary education *or* 20 per cent of the first US$5 000 in tuition fees per family, net of any federal educational aid. The tax break is phased out at about US$70 000 to US$100 000 in income. Further, taxpayers can exclude from income up to US$5 250 of employer-provided education assistance, and deduct some or all interest paid on student loans during the first 60 months of repayment and some contributions into savings plans for tertiary education expenses. Investment income in these plans is subject to no or deferred tax. Taxpayers can claim as dependents all family members who are 18 to 24 years of age and enrolled full-time.

while enrolled. Under a distinctive "study right" policy in New Zealand, per student funding to institutions is provided at 95 per cent of the base rate for students who are under 22-years-old and enrolling for the first time in tertiary education, with eligibility extending up to three years. Students who do not meet the criteria are funded at 75 per cent of the base rate. Some institutions, but not all, differentiate fees according to the level of study right funding. The policy is under review, partly because institutions that cater to target populations receive relatively less funding.

In those countries where parents are expected to contribute toward the costs of their children's education, a trend has been to extend that responsibility further into the student's young adult years, to age 24 in Australia, New Zealand and the United States and to age 26 in Austria. Those students in their early twenties who do not receive parental support face higher costs, and therefore may choose to delay participation until they can establish financial independence. In other countries, such as Finland and Denmark, students are considered financially independent of parents. Another policy which affects the costs faced by adults is the treatment of social welfare benefits of students, including unemployment insurance. In Denmark and Norway, beneficiaries retain this support during studies (in Denmark for two years), although they receive greatly reduced student financial aid. As benefits generally are greater than subsidies provided to students, this policy eliminates a potential disincentive to commence or return to tertiary-level studies. However, the calculations may differ under particular circumstances, so that a single policy may lead to higher costs for some adults and lower costs for others.

Academic achievement

Tertiary education finance policies may work to impose higher costs on students other than the most academically prepared, able and talented, in direct and indirect ways. Students other than the highest achievers comprise a growing proportion of the intake into tertiary education, as participation rates in tertiary-level studies approach half or more of each generation. More and more individuals with a wider range of talents, interests and capabilities now aspire to

and enter tertiary education. Policies will need to take these differences into account, to a greater degree and perhaps in new ways.

At present, in Germany and the United States among other countries, those with higher academic achievement compete for a limited volume of merit awards and, if successful in the competition, incur lower costs than other students. In Japan and also in Portugal, overall tuition fee and financing policies work in the same direction. Demand for places in public universities in these countries exceeds the number of funded places, which means that admission is restricted to higher achievers. The result is that students other than the top academic achievers who aspire to university studies have as their only option private universities, which charge tuition fees closer to full cost. In Japan, the relevant policies are under review or being revised in ways which will extend public funding to students other than the highest academic achievers. The ongoing university reform seeks to widen the criteria for selection, thus weakening the reliance on narrow achievement tests for admission.

A number of countries, including Austria, Finland, France, the Netherlands, Norway, Sweden and the United States, apply rules that increase fees or reduce financial support for students who do not maintain steady progress toward a given qualification. Such policies may work to the disadvantage of all but the most directed and high achieving students. Others who are qualified but also bring different capacities and talents may require somewhat more time to complete course-work or decide that a new programme orientation will better suit their needs. Although policies vary in detail and may not be applied rigidly, most countries now provide less flexibility and impose higher costs on those who require more time: in Austria as in Belgium (Flanders), financial aid is withdrawn if a student fails to complete successfully a defined part of a course in a given period; in Denmark, students may draw on their eligibility for financial aid for the number of months corresponding to the prescribed duration of their chosen study programme, plus twelve months. In a number of other countries, including the Netherlands and Finland, financial support is also time-limited. (Details on the programmes in these two countries can be found in Box 4.2.)

For individual students, differences in costs will depend on a greater range of factors than those described above. First of all, some individuals will be faced with a combination of the characteristics that affect the costs to be covered. For example, a part-time student who is also of mature age could have two cost disadvantages compounded.

A second factor adding to cost differences is the fact that course lengths vary. First degree/diploma programmes can range from two to five years or more in duration, and some students take longer than the prescribed time to complete, for a variety of reasons. In France, ten different pathways through tertiary education are followed by those pursuing an advanced specialised qualification, the *Diplôme d'études supérieures spécialisées* (DESS), to complete their studies (Observatoire des coûts, 1997). Owing to differences in the duration of studies arising from the types of course followed, to changes in orientation and to the need to delay or retake courses at each of three stages (*cycles*) leading to the DESS, student earnings actually used to cover education-related and living costs could vary from one student to another by more than 40 per cent. The differences are important, as student earnings account for about a quarter of resources from all sources which students have available to meet such costs.[7]

It is important to consider individual circumstances when deciding on time limits for student support. It is understandable that governments restrict in many cases the amount of public subsidy allocated to any one student. But the design of funding arrangements needs to avoid the assumption that every student will follow a preset pathway determined by governments. Students have different needs and interests, and the funding system should be sensitive to this – aiming to provide flexible opportunities rather than assuming that each student will follow a traditional route. The French case clearly shows that flexibility is not always without financial cost, and in the United States and other countries delays are often associated with a failure to complete a study programme.[8] But in redesigning financing arrangements, the study combinations desired by learners and needed in the economy and society need to be taken into account.

A key implication is the need to take a fresh look at structures for financing tertiary education. Financing arrangements largely adapted from those in place when there was "less traffic" in and less diversity of demand for tertiary education seem less able to respond to the volume and patterns of participation, characteristics and circumstances of learners and the diversity of learning aims. To strengthen the opportunities of potential students to make informed decisions about the choices, greater transparency is needed not only on the different types, settings and timing of studies but also on their respective costs and on the amounts and forms of financial support available. Beyond this, tuition fee and financial aid policy should introduce greater neutrality among tertiary education study options.

4. **RESPONSE TO INCENTIVES**

New financing strategies aim not only to mobilise needed resources from a wider range of public and private sources but also to influence student behaviour in ways that make tertiary education more cost-effective. The aim is to provide wide access to a range of study options while encouraging students to move more rapidly to complete their study programmes. One way of assessing the success of these strategies is to look at how learners respond to various incentives.

It is hard to determine the precise impact of the level of student and family payments for tuition on learner behaviour, partly because the payments cannot be seen in isolation from other "visible" costs as well as grants, tax expenditures and other subsidies and partly because a host of other factors come into play. Thus, countries in which students and their families pay more to tertiary education institutions have participation rates which vary

---

7. Estimates by the OECD Secretariat. The duration of studies leading to the DESS ranges from 5 to 7.29 years, depending on the pathway followed (Observatoire des coûts, 1997). On average, student earnings account for 25.6 per cent of estimated direct and in-kind resources available for education-related and living costs (Eicher and Gruel, 1996).

8. It is difficult to interpret data on rates of completion of study programmes. For a variety of reasons, students may choose to extend the duration of their studies through alternating periods of work or other activities and formal learning. Not all students undertaking tertiary-level studies seek a degree or diploma. See OECD (1997a and 1998).

widely (Figure 4.4a). For a group of countries, there is a very weak tendency for higher household payments to be associated with short completion times (Figure 4.4b). Such associations as can be observed must be treated with considerable caution, as many factors influence participation and study duration.

Looked at from another angle, students can be used as a vehicle for allocating public funds to tertiary education institutions and, through this means, introduce an incentive for programmes and teaching to be organised in ways that meet student needs and so reduce the costs of failure and mismatches. Public funding of institutions based directly on student enrolments, already in place in the majority of OECD countries, provides such an incentive. The incentive is more transparent when public funds, in the form of student financial aid, augment the funds provided by students and their families. But, as shown in Figure 4.5, there is no close correspondence between the level of payments of students, from their own means or through student financial aid, and average programme costs.

These patterns should not necessarily be taken to mean that payments by or through students and their families have no incentive effects. There is evidence that net costs can influence the enrolment decisions of young people from low income families and there is some indication that adults also are sensitive to costs when making enrolment decisions. Available data in several countries indicate that participation rates from low income or lower class families have not increased with expansion. In the United States, the participation rate of young people from the lowest income quartile changed very little from the late 1970s into the mid-1990s, while that of the highest income quartile rose by 10 per cent. In Japan, after strong increases through the 1970s, the representation of students from the lowest income quintile did not increase over the 1980s and is judged, by some analysts, to be below their share in the population (Kaneko and Kitamura, 1995). In some contrast, students from working class families in the United Kingdom apparently increased their representation in full-time first-degree and diploma courses, in the fifteen years to 1993 (Smithers and Robinson, 1995).

Figure 4.4a
Household contributions to costs and participation rate

Figure 4.4b
Household contributions to costs and average duration of studies

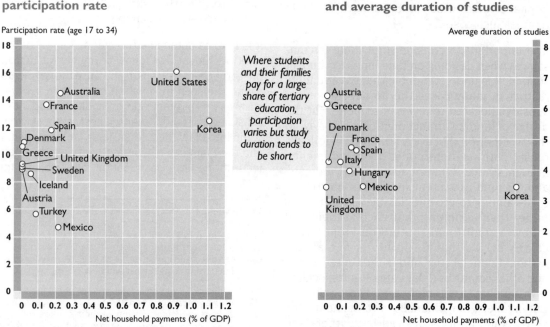

Where students and their families pay for a large share of tertiary education, participation varies but study duration tends to be short.

Source: OECD Education Database.
Data for Figure 4.4: page 82.

Figure 4.5
Expenditure per student over the average duration of studies and final sources of funds for tertiary education institutions, 1994

Expenditure per student over
the average duration of studies

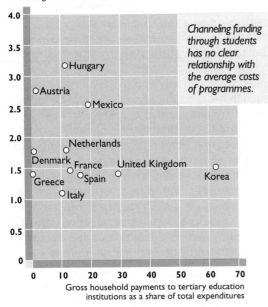

Channeling funding through students has no clear relationship with the average costs of programmes.

Gross household payments to tertiary education
institutions as a share of total expenditures

Source: OECD Education Database.
Data for Figure 4.5: page 82.

A host of factors account for these patterns, so it is not easy to separate out the role played by the costs faced by students and families of limited means. In this respect, recent Australian experience provides a good case study: the numbers of students of low socio-economic status (SES) have increased in proportion to the 30 per cent growth in enrolment over the first half of the 1990s, but their share of enrolment in 1996 stood at 15.5 per cent, about the same as in 1990 (Meek, 1998). Over this period, a Higher Education Contribution charge was introduced, with revenues earmarked for tertiary education. However the scheme allows students to defer payment until they leave tertiary education and payments are linked to income. So the need to marshal additional resources at the time of enrolment apparently would not have slowed the rate of growth in participation of students from low SES families. Other factors may play a decisive role. Students from such backgrounds may be averse

to taking on an obligation for deferred payment, against an unfamiliar if not uncertain prospect for improved employment and earnings later. Where young adults from low SES families use their earnings to cover family expenses, greater subsidies may be required to encourage and enable participation.

A substantial body of research in the United States confirms that changes in net costs to students from low income families do affect the likelihood of enrolment and, further, that these students may be the most sensitive to such changes (see, *e.g.*, McPherson and Schapiro, 1991). The finding is important, pointing to the need to investigate and to take account of the consequences of seeking greater participation of students and families in financing tertiary education.

Finally, where there has been a shift from grants to loans to finance student tuition fees, charges or living costs, the impact of prospective and actual debt and repayment obligations is far from clear. Students respond in part by taking on part-time work. In many countries, a high proportion of full-time students have employment. Some countries and institutions recognise that this development needs not just to be taken into account but potentially used to good advantage: well-managed work experiences can complement a student's learning experiences. Nonetheless, the scale of student debt is increasing in some countries: in Canada, for example, the average debt load of a graduate is expected to increase from Can$ 13 000 in 1990 to Can$ 25 000 in 1999 when the proportion of borrowers with debts larger that Can$ 15 000 will reach 40 per cent. New measures to help manage student debt provide a tax credit on interest payments and introduce changes in the Canada Student Loans programme for interest write-off, extended repayment and partial debt reduction for those with relatively low incomes.

Loan financing does not occur in isolation, but is linked to other individual and family consumption, investment and savings decisions over the lifecycle. There are important implications for the implementation of a lifelong approach to learning: families which, on the margin, would have spent money for early childhood education or additional out-of-school enrichment to complement school instruction may be more likely to set money aside for the payment of fees for tertiary education. Even where the repayment of loans is income-contingent, adults who are repaying them may have fewer resources to spare for their own further learning or for their children's early educational experiences. These choices arise out of a new balance between, on the one hand, enhanced incomes for a large share of a generation which gives greater capacity to absorb additional expenses, and on the other a new obligation spread widely in the population to pay or repay the costs of tertiary education. How the shift in the sharing of the costs of tertiary education – from the public (or parent) to the learner – is realised may be as important as *what* those shares will be.

5. **CONCLUSIONS**

It is not easy to encapsulate, using presently available data, the complex ways in which students and their families are investing money in tertiary education. But it is clear that an analysis of the way tertiary education is financed needs to look at who pays what for learning, not just at the funding level of institutions. A preliminary conclusion is that many students are investing resources in their own learning, and may well become more effective learners as a result of having this financial stake. But, it is important that incentives are not skewed in ways that reduce the study opportunities for some groups. The most obvious is low-income households, whose members have never participated much in tertiary education and could be further put off by rising private costs. But it is also important to consider the rationale for existing structures that may unduly favour students who go down a particular well-established track, rather than those who wish to pursue pathways more precisely geared to their own needs. As far as possible, governments should aim to permit these pathways to be planned across a "level playing field", in which undue obstacles do not arbitrarily determine the route. ■

References

DEPARTMENT FOR EMPLOYMENT, EDUCATION, TRAINING AND YOUTH AFFAIRS – DEETYA (1998), *Learning for Life*, Canberra.

EICHER, J.C. and **GRUEL, L.** (1996), "Le financement de la vie étudiante", Cahiers de l'Observatoire de la Vie Etudiante, No. 3, La Documentation Française, Paris.

JOHNSTONE, D. B. (1985), *Sharing the Costs of Higher Education*, The College Board, New York.

KANEKO, M. and **KITAMURA, K.** (1995), "Towards mass higher education: Access and participation. Country case study – Japan", Mimeo, Ministry of Education, Science and Culture, Tokyo.

MCPHERSON, M.S. and **SCHAPIRO, M.O.** (1991), *Keeping College Affordable: Government and Educational Opportunity*, The Brookings Institution, Washington, D.C.

MEEK, L. (1998), *Managing Education Diversity in a Climate of Public Sector Reform*, Canberra.

OBSERVATOIRE DES COÛTS DES ÉTABLISSEMENTS DE L'ENSEIGNEMENT SUPÉRIEUR (1997), *Les DESS scientifiques : Quels parcours diplômants? Quels coûts?*, Presses Universitaires de Grenoble.

OECD (1995), *Continuing Professional Education of Highly-Qualified Personnel*, Paris.

OECD (1997a), *Education Policy Analysis 1997*, Paris.

OECD (1997b), *Education at a Glance – OECD Indicators 1997*, Paris.

OECD (1998), *Redefining Tertiary Education*, Paris.

SMITHERS, A. and **ROBINSON, P.** (1995), *Post-18 Education: Growth, Change, Prospect*, The Council for Industry and Higher Education, London.

STATISTICAL ANNEX
Data for the figures

Chapter 1

Data for Figures 1.1 and 1.3
Participation in education and training[1] over the life-span: country variations

▨ Enrolment in formal education
▨ Participation in adult education and training

	3-5	6-7	8-12	13-15	16-18	19-21	22-24	25-29	30-34	35-39	40-44	45-49	50-54	55-59	60-65
									Age groups						
Belgium	97.65	96.65	95.86	96.56	91.64	56.15	22.44	8.91							
					0.00*	18.31*	26.26*	25.87	24.63	22.39	22.08	23.09	22.65	16.49*	9.17*
					(0.00)	(9.69)	(5.63)	(3.24)	(3.19)	(1.81)	(2.74)	(3.44)	(2.98)	(3.38)	(2.34)
Canada	47.71	100.33	100.09	98.99	78.22	49.13	24.27	10.10							
					78.41	63.16	51.02	48.68	40.63	40.28	43.62	29.75	33.99	27.05	10.09
					(4.46)	(6.76)	(4.97)	(5.03)	(4.82)	(6.44)	(3.87)	(7.09)	(6.95)	(6.11)	(2.94)
Ireland	50.73	100.42	100.34	98.22	81.77	34.96	12.95	7.16							
					37.06*	36.70	33.12	30.29	26.41	28.37	22.33	19.49	19.58	12.59*	5.41*
					(10.31)	(4.81)	(5.97)	(5.00)	(3.32)	(5.16)	(3.31)	(4.15)	(5.12)	(4.10)	(1.87)
Netherlands	65.19	99.36	99.34	99.08	91.30	58.66	29.69	11.23							
					41.22*	42.19*	57.09	49.41	43.34	42.84	38.65	34.64	29.19	18.00	16.38
					(9.98)	(7.26)	(5.62)	(2.60)	(2.38)	(2.90)	(2.77)	(2.94)	(3.23)	(3.18)	(2.95)
New Zealand	95.48	100.00	100.00	98.99	77.28	47.89	19.72	10.72							
					79.40	66.55	61.48	55.26	50.29	51.71	49.70	44.42	45.96	36.21	18.53
					(5.00)	(5.70)	(4.97)	(2.83)	(2.54)	(3.06)	(2.27)	(3.33)	(4.47)	(5.46)	(3.64)
Sweden	57.24	94.30	100.41	98.46	93.51	32.22	27.45	14.94							
					54.31*	43.58	45.87	56.06	55.30	59.49	62.88	57.07	58.82	48.01	25.43
					(11.23)	(6.76)	(3.69)	(2.55)	(3.88)	(3.79)	(2.74)	(3.48)	(3.32)	(2.99)	(2.45)
Switzerland[2]	36.87	99.60	99.84	98.64	82.48	38.10	19.25	9.32							
					32.34*	60.70*	50.05*	55.85	47.46	42.86	46.94	41.87	36.38	29.45	22.16
					(8.26)	(8.45)	(5.72)	(3.01)	(3.05)	(3.81)	(5.16)	(3.72)	(3.43)	(3.50)	(4.09)
United Kingdom[3]	79.07	99.17	98.75	98.51	71.60	38.83	17.57	10.98							
					71.35	53.55	57.28	55.79	51.87	51.05	56.63	47.22	35.14	29.60	16.26
					(6.02)	(5.15)	(4.69)	(2.36)	(2.41)	(3.15)	(3.37)	(2.73)	(3.30)	(2.32)	(2.52)
United States	65.00	100.00	100.00	100.00	75.01	37.49	22.93	11.72							
					44.68	47.76	49.86	46.56	45.03	44.65	47.37	45.56	42.51	34.34	19.52
					(10.15)	(11.62)	(6.84)	(3.34)	(4.13)	(3.23)	(2.55)	(2.73)	(3.24)	(4.79)	(3.24)
Country mean[4]	66.10	98.87	99.40	98.61	82.54	43.72	21.81	10.56							
					48.75	48.06	48.00	47.09	42.77	42.63	43.35	38.12	36.02	27.97	15.88

* Sample size is insufficient to permit a reliable estimate. Standard errors of estimates in brackets.
1. Adult education and training excludes full-time students aged under 24.
2. Data on adult education and training refer to French and German-speaking parts of Switzerland covered in the International Adult Literacy Survey.
3. Participation in formal education for individuals 22 to 29 years of age is underestimated, because data on enrolment for advanced university programmes are not available by single age.
4. Unweighted mean of net participation, for nine countries: Belgium (Flanders), Canada, Ireland, Netherlands, New Zealand, Sweden, Switzerland (French and German for IALS), United Kingdom, United States.
Sources: OECD Education Database 1995, and International Adult Literacy Survey 1994-1995.

Data for Figure 1.2A
Educational attainment[1] of women compared to men, 25 to 34 and 55 to 64 year-olds, 1995

	Estimated average years of education				Percentage difference[2]	
	25 to 34 year-olds		55 to 64 year-olds		Age 25-34	Age 55-64
	Men	Women	Men	Women		
Australia	13.0	12.6	12.6	12.0	-2.7	-4.9
Austria	12.9	12.4	11.8	10.7	-3.2	-9.4
Belgium	11.1	11.9	9.1	8.4	7.6	-7.2
Denmark	12.7	12.8	12.0	11.1	0.7	-7.0
Finland	12.3	12.4	10.7	10.4	0.9	-2.9
France	12.1	12.2	9.0	8.2	0.7	-8.5
Germany	13.7	13.4	13.6	12.1	-2.2	-10.6
Greece	10.0	11.3	8.2	7.2	12.9	-12.1
Ireland	12.4	13.5	10.4	10.6	8.9	2.5
Italy	10.4	10.9	7.5	6.6	4.6	-12.3
Netherlands	11.9	12.3	11.3	9.9	3.5	-11.9
New Zealand	10.8	11.6	10.7	9.6	8.0	-9.9
Norway	12.4	12.8	11.7	11.2	3.3	-4.0
Portugal	5.5	8.9	7.1	6.7	61.0	-5.2
Spain	10.0	11.4	7.4	6.8	13.7	-7.7
Sweden	12.3	12.5	10.0	10.1	1.2	1.4
Switzerland	13.9	13.0	13.5	11.8	-6.2	-12.9
United Kingdom	14.2	14.0	13.2	12.3	-1.3	-6.7
United States	12.5	12.8	12.3	11.9	3.0	-3.1

1. Educational attainment is the sum of the number of persons having attained a given level of education in the age and gender group, weighted by the typical duration of studies at that level in the country concerned. The typical duration of studies at each level is taken from OECD (1997), Education at a Glance – OECD Indicators 1997, Table X.1.1, p. 347.
2. Percentage difference is calculated for each group as the difference between mean educational attainment for women and men, divided by mean educational attainment for men, multiplied by 100.
Source: OECD Education Database.

Data for Figure 1.2B

Participation in adult education and training[1] of women compared to men, 25 to 34 and 55 to 64 year-olds, 1994-95

	25 to 34 year-olds				55 to 64 year-olds				Percentage difference	
	Men		Women		Men		Women		Age 25-34	Age 55-64
Belgium (Flanders)	24.6	(3.2)	25.1	(2.5)	14.0*	(3.5)	11.4*	(2.2)	2.2	-18.1
Canada	48.1	(4.1)	39.1	(4.4)	18.2	(7.7)	18.4	(6.5)	-18.8	1.1
Ireland	26.0	(3.9)	29.9	(3.1)	9.7*	(2.7)	8.3*	(2.0)	15.0	-14.2
Netherlands	50.5	(2.6)	42.0	(2.1)	12.6*	(2.7)	20.0	(3.1)	-16.9	58.0
New Zealand	46.7	(3.2)	38.5	(2.1)	23.1	(4.5)	21.7	(3.0)	-17.5	-6.0
Sweden	57.0	(3.7)	54.3	(3.7)	36.3	(3.0)	39.3	(2.1)	-4.6	8.2
Switzerland[2]	54.2	(2.8)	45.9	(3.8)	28.3	(4.0)	22.1	(3.9)	-15.3	-22.0
United Kingdom	56.6	(2.7)	50.7	(1.9)	23.2	(2.4)	23.6	(3.2)	-10.4	1.6
United States	43.7	(5.0)	44.3	(3.8)	22.8	(3.6)	31.3	(4.4)	1.2	37.3

* Sample size is insufficient to permit a reliable estimate. Standard errors of estimates in brackets.
1. Participation rate.
2. Data on adult education and training refer to French and German-speaking parts of Switzerland covered in the International Adult Literacy Survey.
Source: International Adult Literacy Survey, 1994-1995.

Data for Figure 1.4

Pre-school participation, 1995

	Net enrolment of	
	3-year-olds	4-year-olds
Australia	18.35	58.42
Austria	30.42	70.66
Belgium	98.47	99.54
Canada	–	47.68
Czech Republic	62.77	74.52
Denmark	59.95	78.77
Finland	26.88	29.49
France	99.50	100.00
Germany	46.61	71.02
Greece	12.68	54.15
Hungary	66.02	87.34
Iceland	77.49	82.85
Ireland	0.86	52.77
Japan	57.64	93.41
Korea	10.41	27.63
Mexico	10.40	52.45
Netherlands	–	97.18
New Zealand	83.27	97.33
Norway	54.49	65.16
Portugal	40.36	55.60
Spain	57.38	100.00
Sweden	51.00	57.61
Switzerland	5.87	26.97
United Kingdom[1]	40.59	10.64
United States	34.18	61.95

–: not applicable, as education is provided from age 4.
1. Over 80 per cent of 4 year-olds in the United Kingdom are already enrolled, beyond pre-school, in primary education.
Source: OECD Education Database.

Data for Figure 1.5

Teenage participation,[1] 1995

	Participation of	
	14-17 year-olds	18-19 year-olds
Australia	97	59
Austria	94	49
Belgium	100	81
Canada	92	57
Czech Republic	92	34
Denmark	93	63
Finland	95	61
France	96	77
Germany	97	75
Greece	78	46
Hungary	88	38
Ireland	92	60
Japan	99	n.a.
Korea	94	48
Luxembourg	80	62
Mexico	49	20
Netherlands	97	76
New Zealand	94	52
Norway	96	66
Portugal	81	50
Spain	88	58
Sweden	97	62
Switzerland	92	67
Turkey	43	17
United Kingdom	90	49
United States	93	49

n.a.: Data not available.
1. Unweighted mean.
Source: OECD Education Database.

Data for Figure 1.6

Towards universal participation of youth in education, 1985 and 1995
Percentage of 14 to 17 year-olds in education

	1985	1995
Austria[1]	86.6	94.5
Belgium	91.8	100.0
Canada	92.5	92.5
Denmark	90.4	92.9
Finland	90.1	95.4
Netherlands	93.0	97.4
New Zealand	74.1	93.7
Norway	90.0	96.1
Portugal	46.2	80.6
Spain	67.3	88.1
Sweden	91.5	97.1
Switzerland	88.5	91.8
United Kingdom[1]	77.8	89.6
United States	92.0	93.0

1. As tertiary education is not included, data for 1985 are slightly underestimated.
Source: OECD Education Database.

Table I.A

Participation in organised adult education and training, 1994-95, selected characteristics (percentages)

	Gender		Employment status			Employer	Firm size		Participation in adult education and training		
	Male	Female	Employed	Unemployed	Inactive	sponsored	Less than 99	100 and over	Less than 1 week	2 weeks	More than 2 weeks
Belgium (Flanders)	24.1	19.4	27.1	15.5	10.0	48.7	21.6	31.9	76.1	13.8	10.2
	(1.7)	(1.2)	(1.3)	(3.3)	(1.7)	(3.1)	(1.8)	(2.0)	(3.6)	(2.3)	(2.6)
Canada	39.8	38.2	44.8	32.3	23.9	45.7	40.7	46.3	59.7	13.1	27.2
	(2.0)	(2.9)	(2.7)	(8.2)	(4.7)	(3.7)	(2.7)	(4.0)	(3.1)	(2.6)	(3.3)
Ireland	23.1	25.8	31.5	15.2	15.5	40.5	24.5	39.7	61.1	9.4	29.5
	(2.7)	(2.2)	(2.7)	(3.7)	(2.3)	(2.5)	(2.8)	(3.2)	(2.5)	(2.0)	(2.2)
Netherlands	39.7	36.1	44.4	37.8	23.4	50.7	n.a.	n.a.	67.1	12.3	20.6
	(1.6)	(1.3)	(1.3)	(5.1)	(2.0)	(1.6)	n.a.	n.a.	(1.4)	(1.3)	(1.4)
New Zealand	50.6	48.4	56.5	37.9	29.9	53.0	47.2	67.2	64.1	8.4	27.4
	(1.7)	(1.5)	(1.4)	(5.0)	(2.4)	(1.6)	(2.0)	(1.7)	(1.7)	(1.0)	(1.6)
Poland	15.7	13.0	20.6	9.4	3.2	59.3	16.5	24.4	73.3	11.8	14.9
	(1.2)	(1.2)	(1.5)	(2.2)	(0.7)	(2.6)	(1.7)	(1.6)	(3.8)	(2.1)	(2.9)
Sweden	51.1	54.0	59.5	44.0	27.2	n.a.	n.a.	n.a.	n.a.	n.a.	n.a.
	(1.4)	(1.6)	(1.3)	(5.6)	(2.7)	n.a.	n.a.	n.a.	n.a.	n.a.	n.a.
Switzerland[1]	44.2	41.2	46.4	34.6	28.3	43.0	40.9	51.5	77.2	10.3	12.6
	(1.8)	(1.9)	(1.3)	(6.5)	(2.2)	(1.5)	(1.7)	(1.6)	(1.4)	(1.3)	(0.9)
United Kingdom	47.8	45.7	58.3	35.7	14.7	67.7	44.1	65.9	66.7	10.0	23.3
	(1.6)	(1.1)	(1.2)	(2.9)	(1.7)	(1.3)	(2.8)	(1.4)	(1.8)	(1.4)	(1.3)
United States	42.7	42.1	49.5	27.9	17.3	60.3	37.3	57.5	76.0	9.2	14.9
	(2.4)	(1.8)	(1.9)	(2.7)	(1.9)	(2.1)	(2.0)	(2.1)	(1.9)	(1.1)	(2.1)

Standard error of estimates in brackets.
n.a.: Data not available.
1. Data on adult education and training refer to French and German-speaking parts of Switzerland covered in the International Adult Literacy Survey.
Source: International Adult Literacy Survey, 1994-1995.

Table I.B

Net enrolment rates[1] by single year of age, 1995

	Age																										
	3	4	5	6	7	8	9	10	11	12	13	14	15	16	17	18	19	20	21	22	23	24	25	26	27	28	29
Australia	18.3	58.4	92.1	100.0	100.0	100.0	99.5	99.7	99.2	100.0	99.6	100.0	98.1	96.0	93.5	65.7	52.8	46.7	33.8	26.1	22.3	20.4	18.7	17.4	15.8	14.8	14.3
Austria	30.4	70.7	90.2	98.8	98.6	100.0	100.0	99.0	98.4	98.8	100.0	100.0	96.6	93.6	87.7	62.5	35.7	25.8	22.1	17.9	16.3	14.9	15.1	12.1	10.2	8.3	6.9
Belgium	98.5	99.5	99.7	100.0	99.4	99.3	99.5	99.6	99.0	99.5	99.7	99.7	100.0	100.0	100.0	87.5	75.3	66.7	49.2	38.1	27.6	19.9	14.9	11.9	9.7	7.9	6.5
Canada	0.0	47.7	96.8	100.0	100.0	99.7	99.9	100.0	100.0	100.0	100.0	98.6	98.1	94.0	79.1	61.9	52.6	50.4	43.4	31.8	23.6	17.9	14.1	11.4	9.7	8.5	7.4
Czech Republic	62.8	74.5	92.7	100.0	100.0	100.0	100.0	100.0	100.0	100.0	100.0	100.0	98.7	96.9	71.7	41.9	26.1	20.3	20.1	18.1	11.1	5.1	3.1	2.5	2.2	2.0	1.6
Denmark	60.0	78.8	82.3	96.9	99.8	99.9	100.0	99.8	99.8	99.7	99.8	98.3	97.8	93.8	81.7	71.7	55.2	42.4	39.8	35.9	32.5	27.9	23.3	18.8	14.4	11.2	9.2
Finland	26.9	29.5	35.0	57.7	99.7	99.6	99.5	99.5	99.5	99.5	99.3	99.3	99.4	92.6	90.5	81.2	41.5	42.9	48.6	43.8	38.7	31.9	26.4	21.0	17.2	14.3	11.6
Germany	46.6	71.0	79.2	86.9	99.3	98.7	99.1	99.4	98.2	98.2	98.5	97.9	98.0	96.9	93.4	84.2	65.3	45.1	33.5	30.5	25.2	21.4	18.5	15.5	13.2	9.3	10.1
Greece	12.7	54.1	79.4	94.4	94.1	95.9	96.6	100.0	100.0	100.0	97.8	91.0	86.1	79.0	55.8	47.8	45.0	36.3	29.4	17.4	12.9	7.8	8.3	5.9	4.9	2.2	1.7
Hungary	66.0	87.3	97.3	98.9	100.0	100.0	99.5	100.0	100.0	99.4	100.0	98.6	93.1	88.2	71.1	46.3	29.9	25.0	18.1	14.7	11.6	8.4	6.2	4.6	3.4	2.5	1.9
Ireland	0.9	52.8	98.2	100.0	100.0	100.0	99.4	100.0	99.6	100.0	98.8	98.0	94.4	89.7	80.0	72.9	47.1	37.3	19.7	15.3	12.8	10.5	8.4	6.8	5.5	4.6	3.8
Mexico	10.4	52.5	80.7	100.0	100.0	100.0	100.0	100.0	98.5	91.6	80.8	67.6	52.0	39.4	37.0	24.7	15.4	13.6	11.5	10.2	9.4	9.1	4.1	2.7	2.7	2.7	2.7
Netherlands	0.1	97.6	99.2	99.3	99.4	99.8	99.7	99.7	98.6	98.9	99.0	99.2	99.0	98.3	93.3	82.5	70.1	59.6	47.5	37.6	29.7	22.6	16.5	13.9	10.1	8.3	7.3
New Zealand	83.3	97.4	100.0	100.0	100.0	100.0	100.0	100.0	99.0	100.0	99.0	100.0	97.2	99.9	76.8	56.6	47.8	44.5	39.5	26.2	19.0	15.0	12.4	11.4	10.7	10.2	9.8
Norway	54.5	65.2	71.5	90.6	99.2	98.6	99.3	98.8	99.2	99.1	99.0	99.3	99.8	95.0	90.3	83.0	49.2	43.0	40.8	38.1	33.8	27.1	21.4	16.3	13.1	10.5	8.6
Portugal	0.0	55.6	64.6	100.0	100.0	100.0	100.0	100.0	100.0	100.0	100.0	89.3	87.5	72.8	72.8	55.4	45.1	44.1	47.1	25.3	21.7	17.1	13.6	11.0	8.8	6.6	4.3
Spain	57.4	100.0	100.0	100.0	100.0	100.0	100.0	100.0	100.0	100.0	100.0	100.0	94.2	82.7	74.8	62.9	53.1	49.7	39.8	34.2	24.5	16.5	11.2	7.5	6.0	4.7	3.8
Sweden	51.0	57.6	63.4	92.2	96.5	100.0	100.0	100.0	99.5	99.4	99.7	99.3	96.4	97.0	95.8	87.9	35.3	30.6	30.9	30.1	27.9	24.2	20.6	17.0	14.4	12.6	11.0
Switzerland	5.9	27.0	78.9	98.9	99.8	99.8	99.3	99.7	99.2	99.4	98.7	98.5	96.8	86.0	82.5	76.3	56.2	33.6	24.7	21.4	19.3	17.1	14.0	11.3	8.9	7.2	5.9
Turkey	0.3	1.7	14.3	82.7	92.4	94.0	92.3	89.3	68.6	65.4	63.3	55.7	48.2	40.5	25.7	16.9	16.8	12.1	11.3	9.8	8.0	6.5	5.2	4.3	3.3	3.1	2.7
United Kingdom	44.8	93.4	99.8	99.3	99.0	98.9	98.3	98.7	98.6	99.3	98.7	98.3	98.5	86.9	74.7	53.5	45.1	39.2	32.8	21.6	16.9	14.4	12.6	11.6	10.9	10.2	9.7
United States	34.2	61.9	100.0	99.8	100.0	100.0	100.0	100.0	98.2	99.7	100.0	100.0	98.1	89.9	78.6	55.6	42.0	35.4	35.0	25.1	23.0	20.9	16.2	13.8	11.2	9.9	8.0
Country mean	34.8	65.2	82.5	95.3	99.0	99.3	99.2	99.2	97.9	97.6	96.9	94.9	92.2	86.8	77.6	62.7	45.6	38.4	32.7	25.9	21.3	17.1	13.9	11.3	9.4	7.8	6.8

1. Participation in formal education only; adult education and training is excluded.
Source: OECD Education Database.

Chapter 2

Data for Figure 2.1A
Teaching staff employed in primary and secondary education[1] as a percentage of the total labour force, 1995

(based on head counts)

Hungary	4.2
Belgium (Flanders)	4.1
Italy	3.8
Spain	3.6
Sweden	3.5
Ireland	3.4
Austria	3.2
Denmark[2]	3.2
France	3.1
Mexico	3.0
Greece	2.8
United Kingdom	2.8
New Zealand	2.3
United States	2.3
Turkey	2.2
Canada	2.1
Japan	1.8
Korea	1.7
Country mean	**2.9**

1. Public and private.
2. Estimated.
Source: OECD Education Database.

Data for Figure 2.1B
Percentage of women among teaching staff, by level of education, 1995

	Full-time teaching staff	
	Primary and lower secondary education	Upper secondary education
Hungary	84	55
Italy	84	55
United States	78	50
Sweden	73	42
Austria	72	49
United Kingdom	70	n.a.
New Zealand	69	48
Finland	68	n.a.
Belgium (Flanders)	67	44
Spain	66	48
Denmark[1]	58	45
Greece	58	46
Norway	58	32
Korea	56	25
Germany	52	24
Japan	51	24
Turkey	43	40
Country mean	**65**	**42**

n.a.: Data not available.
1. Estimated.
Source: OECD Education Database.

Data for Figure 2.1C
Annual statutory teachers' salaries at the lower secondary level of education, public institutions, 1995

	Ratio of salary after 15 years' experience to GDP per capita
Korea	2.9
Ireland	2.0
Portugal	2.0
Spain	2.0
Switzerland	2.0
Germany	1.8
Netherlands	1.8
Finland	1.5
Belgium	1.4
France	1.4
New Zealand	1.4
Austria	1.3
Denmark[1]	1.3
Greece	1.3
Italy	1.2
United States	1.2
Sweden	1.1
Norway	0.9
Czech Republic	0.8
Country mean	**1.5**

1. Estimated.
Source: OECD Education Database.

Data for Figure 2.1D
Percentage of teachers by age, primary and secondary education, public and private institutions, 1994-95

	Under 30 years	50 years and over
Iceland[1,2]	21.1	21.1
Portugal[2]	17.4	15.4
Austria	15.1	12.6
Ireland[3,4]	14.4	23.1
Belgium[5,6]	14.0	23.3
Luxembourg[2]	13.6	25.0
United Kingdom	12.5	22.2
France[5]	11.8	21.0
Finland[7]	10.4	28.1
Norway[1,2,4]	9.4	31.0
Sweden	6.2	39.6
Germany[4]	3.2	31.8
Denmark[8]	3.1	26.8
Country mean	**11.7**	**24.7**

1. ISCED 1 to 3, public sector.
2. Public sector only.
3. Including school heads and guidance teachers.
4. Excludes those with age unknown.
5. Including pre-primary.
6. Excluding special education.
7. ISCED 1 to 5, 1995-96.
8. Estimated.
Source: Eurydice (1997), *Key Data on Education in the European Union*, European Communities, Luxembourg, Data for Figures G13, G14 and G15.

Data for Figure 2.2
Computers in schools

	Year	Average number of students per computer
Portugal	1994	50
Japan	1994	50
Finland	1992*	42
	1996*	28
	1996**	18
Sweden	1993*	38
	1993**	10
France	1994	33
Netherlands	1994	33
Denmark	1992	25
	1996	12
Norway	1993	21
	1995**	8
Canada	1994	15
United Kingdom	1994	9
United States	1995	9

....

* Primary and lower secondary schools.
** Upper secondary schools.
Source: OECD (1997), *Information Technology Outlook* 1997, Paris.

Chapter 3

Data for Figure 3.1

Relative size of the youth population, and GDP per capita

	15-24 year-olds as a percentage of the population[1]		GDP per capita 1994 ($)[2] (at PPP exchange rates)
	1998	2008	
Australia	13.9	13.3	18 500
Austria	12.5	12.5	20 200
Belgium	12.3	11.9	20 300
Canada	13.2	13.2	20 300
Czech Republic	16.1	12.7	8 900
Denmark	12.2	11.6	20 400
Finland	12.6	12.3	16 300
France	13.4	12.6	19 200
Germany	11.5	11.8	19 700
Greece	14.2	10.9	11 600
Hungary	15.4	12.6	6 300
Iceland	15.2	14.3	19 300
Ireland	18.4	14.5	15 800
Italy	12.7	11.2	18 600
Japan	13.7	10.3	21 200
Korea	17.4	13.6	10 400
Luxembourg	12.8	12.1	30 100
Mexico	20.9	18.4	7 800
Netherlands	12.0	12.1	18 800
New Zealand	14.5	14.2	16 000
Norway	12.4	12.6	22 000
Poland	16.7	14.7	5 000
Portugal	15.1	11.3	12 000
Spain	15.1	10.7	13 600
Sweden	11.7	12.7	17 600
Switzerland	9.4	11.9	23 900
Turkey	21.2	16.5	5 300
United Kingdom	12.4	12.9	17 600
United States	13.3	14.1	25 500
Country mean (unweighted)	**14.6**	**12.9**	**16 600**

PPP: Purchasing power parities.
1. Projections based on the United Nations population database.
2. OECD (1997), *Education at a Glance* – OECD *Indicators* 1997, Paris.
Source: OECD Databases.

Data for Figure 3.2

Percentage of 20-24 year-olds whose highest level of educational attainment is lower secondary school (ISCED 0-2), 1995 and change from 1989[1]

	1989	1995			Change, 1989-1995
	Total	Total	Men	Women	
Australia	n.a.	32	28	36	n.a.
Austria	20	19	17	22	-1
Belgium	35	22	26	18	-13
Canada	n.a.	16	18	13	3
Czech Republic	n.a.	7	7	8	n.a.
Denmark	n.a.	34	37	30	n.a.
Finland	18	21	21	21	3
France	n.a.	11	11	11	n.a.
Greece	n.a.	26	31	22	n.a.
Ireland	38[2]	26	31	21	-12
Italy	54	31	24	36	-23
Korea	n.a.	6	8	4	n.a.
Netherlands	n.a.	31	35	27	n.a.
New Zealand	n.a.	28	28	29	n.a.
Norway	10	9	9	8	-1
Poland	n.a.	13	15	10	n.a.
Portugal	90	57	64	49	-33
Spain	n.a.	41	46	35	n.a.
Sweden	14	12	11	13	-2
Switzerland	12	19	15	22	7
Turkey	n.a.	65	59	71	n.a.
United Kingdom	19	11	11	11	-8
United States	15	15	16	13	0
Country mean (unweighted)	**30**	**24**	**25**	**23**	**-9**

n.a.: Data not available.
1. The data includes those 20-24 year-olds who are still in upper secondary education. This is a small proportion of the age group in many countries and 15 per cent for the 18 countries in the table for which 1995 data is available. See OECD (1997), *Education at a Glance* – OECD *Indicators* 1997, Paris. However it is relatively high, at 32 and 31 per cent respectively, in the case of the Netherlands and Denmark.
2. Source: National authorities.
Source: OECD Education Database.

Data for Figure 3.3

Percentage of 20-24 year-olds whose highest level of educational attainment is lower secondary school (ISCED 0-2), and percentage of this low attainment group unemployed, 1995

	Percentage of 20-24 year-olds	Percentage who are unemployed
Australia	32	13
Austria	19	5
Belgium	22	19
Canada	16	17
Czech Republic	7	12
Denmark	34	14
Finland	21	24
France	11	27
Greece	26	13
Ireland	26	23
Italy	31	28
Korea	6	3
Netherlands	31	10
New Zealand	28	11
Norway	9	12
Poland	13	21
Portugal	57	11
Spain	41	31
Sweden	12	20
Turkey	65	8
United Kingdom	11	21
United States	15	12
Country mean (unweighted)	**24**	**16**

Source: OECD Education Database.

Data for Figure 3.4

Average number of years spent employed over the first five years after leaving initial education by persons whose highest level of education attainment is lower secondary education

Men[1]

Highest educational attainment	Years spent employed (% of group)						Total %	Average years (weighted)
	Never employed	1 year	2 years	3 years	4 years	5 years		
Lower secondary								
Australia	8	7	14	17	16	37	100	3.4
France	3	6	10	12	22	47	100	3.9
Germany	2	3	2	7	21	66	100	4.4
Ireland	7	4	6	13	15	55	100	3.9
United States	8	9	12	19	22	31	100	3.3
Upper secondary								
Australia	4	5	6	15	17	52	100	3.9
France[2]	..	..	..	..	..	..	..	..
Germany	0	2	2	3	12	81	100	4.7
Ireland	2	2	4	9	28	53	100	4.2
United States	3	5	8	13	22	48	100	3.9
Tertiary								
Australia	5	4	4	8	13	66	100	4.2
France[3]	7	5	19	38	32	..	100	2.8
Germany	0	0	0	5	25	70	100	4.7
Ireland[4]	12	5	16	66	..	..	100	2.4
United States	1	1	2	4	17	76	100	4.7

Women[1]

Highest educational attainment	Years spent employed (% of group)						Total %	Average years (weighted)
	Never employed	1 year	2 years	3 years	4 years	5 years		
Lower secondary								
Australia	37	13	7	5	8	30	100	2.2
France	5	9	11	12	15	48	100	3.7
Germany	8	2	6	5	33	45	100	3.9
Ireland	17	8	10	14	8	43	100	3.2
United States	29	25	13	16	11	6	100	1.7
Upper secondary								
Australia	6	6	6	10	19	53	100	3.9
France[2]	..	..	..	..	..	..	..	..
Germany	1	2	8	6	21	63	100	4.3
Ireland	2	3	5	9	30	51	100	4.2
United States	8	9	13	13	20	36	100	3.3
Tertiary								
Australia	2	11	8	13	13	52	100	3.8
France[3]	4	4	7	22	64	..	100	3.4
Germany	5	2	0	9	28	56	100	4.2
Ireland[4]	2	3	16	80	..	..	100	2.7
United States	3	3	5	10	19	60	100	4.2

1. The data are based on national longitudinal studies that collect data annually. The analysis is based on dating labour market entry as the first interview in which individuals report that they are not in education, and then retaining these people in the analysis so long as over subsequent periods they do not report being enrolled in education. Due to differing methodologies and time periods, the date of permanent entry to the labour market varies, for example, 1981-1988 for the United States and 1989-1990 for Australia. It is likely that the period of entry affects the probability of gaining employment. The reporting of employment status is taken at the time of each annual survey. Thus, the number of persons with some months employed is understated, and the number with some months unemployed is overstated. Persons leaving education at different stages will vary in their age, for example the difference in leaving age between those who leave after compulsory schooling and those who leave after university could be 10 years or more. Countries differ in the proportion of education leavers from each stage of education. For example, in the United States only 10 per cent of education leavers have a highest level of educational attainment of lower secondary, whereas the corresponding proportion for Germany is about 30 per cent. Full details on the data sources and the care needed in their interpretation are provided in OECD (1998), "Getting started, setting in: The transition from education to the labour market", *Employment Outlook* 1998, Paris.
2. There are no French data for leavers from upper secondary education.
3. The French data for tertiary graduates refer to the first four years since leaving education.
4. The Irish data for tertiary graduates refer to the first three years since leaving education.
Source: OECD (1998), "Getting started, setting in: The transition from education to the labour market", *Employment Outlook* 1998, Paris.

Data for Figure 3.5

Service sector employment as a proportion of total employment, youth and adults, early 1990s

	Aged 15-24 years (%)	Aged 25 years and over (%)
Australia, 1994	75	70
Finland, 1993	69	66
Germany, 1992	60	58
Italy, 1991	47	59
United States, 1993	80	72

Source: OECD Education Database.

Data for Figure 3.6
Pathways from compulsory schooling to the labour market and further education, and selected outcomes in four countries, 1995

A. Pathways from compulsory schooling to work and further education

	Typical entry age	Percentage of cohort entering the pathway after compulsory education	Duration (years)	Destination(s) for which pathway qualifies young people
General education				
Australia	16	83	2	Tertiary study[1]
Austria	15	20	4	Tertiary study[1]
Czech Republic	15	16	4	Tertiary study[1]
Norway	16	47	3	Tertiary study[1]
School-based vocational				
Australia	16	2[2]	0.5 - 2	Work
Austria – pathway to work & study[3]	15	23[4]	5	Work & study
Austria – pathway to work	15	14[4]	3-4	Work
Czech Republic – pathway to work & study[3]	15	41	2-4	Work & study
Czech Republic – pathway to work[5]	15	39	1-4	Work
Norway	16	26[6,7]	3	Work & study
Apprenticeship-type				
Australia	16-18	3[2]	1-4	Work
Austria	15	40[8]	3-4	Work
Czech Republic	–	–	–	Work
Norway	16	24[7]	4	Work & study

Percentage of 16-year-olds (or grade equivalent) not in education or training

Australia	12
Austria	3
Czech Republic	2 (15-year-olds)
Norway	3

–: not applicable.
1. In each country the principal structural link from the general education pathway is to tertiary education. Nevertheless, many of those who complete general education do not enter tertiary study, but enter the labour market or other activities. The estimated proportions who do so immediately following the end of the general education pathway are: Australia, 50 per cent; Austria, under 10 per cent; Czech Republic, 10 per cent; Norway, 50 per cent.
2. Flows from the general education pathway in Australia to the two vocational pathways increase during and after upper secondary education, so that by age 18-19 some 20 per cent of the cohort are involved in vocational pathways.
3. Austria and the Czech Republic each offer two school-based vocational education pathways, one allowing young people to qualify both for tertiary education and for work, and the other allowing them to qualify for work. In the Czech Republic, only a small minority of students in this pathway undertake two or three-year programmes. Those who wish to qualify for tertiary study must take the four-year programme.
4. Periods of work experience are compulsory in each of the two school-based vocational pathways in Austria.
5. Three years is the most common pattern of study in this pathway. Some students in the pathway undertake a fourth year of study and by doing so can qualify for tertiary study.
6. Periods of work experience are compulsory in some but not all school-based vocational pathways in Norway.
7. Perhaps a quarter of those who commence the vocational pathways in Norway subsequently transfer to general education. Those who complete a vocational pathway can qualify for tertiary study by an additional six months of general education.
8. About a third of those who commence an apprenticeship in Austria have transferred from other pathways, predominantly the two school-based vocational pathways.
Source: OECD Secretariat, based on national reports.

B. Selected education and employment outcomes

	Proportion not participating in education at age 18	Unemployment to population ratio, age 20-24
Australia	34	10
Austria	38	3
Czech Republic	58	3
Norway	17	7

Sources: OECD (1997), *Education at a Glance – OECD Indicators 1997*, and OECD Education Database.

Data for Figure 3.7
Percentage of 15-24 year-olds who are unemployed, who are seeking their first job, or who have been unemployed for 12 months or more

	Unemployment rate, 15-24 year-olds[1]	Unemployment to population ratio, 15-24 year-olds[2]	Percentage of the 15-24 unemployed seeking their first job	Percentage of the 15-24 unemployed who have been unemployed for 12 months or more
Austria	6	3	23	14
Belgium	24	9	58	44
Denmark	10	7	13	9
Finland	38	20	75	24
France	27	10	31	24
Germany	9	5	21	27
Greece	28	10	75	50
Ireland	20	9	45	48
Italy	33	13	76	63
Netherlands	12	7	57	33
Portugal	17	7	42	41
Spain	43	18	45	46
Sweden	19	9	20	15
United Kingdom	16	10	31	27
14 EU *countries* mean[3] (weighted)	**22**	**10**	**47**	**40**

1. Percentage of 15-24 year-olds in the labour force who are unemployed.
2. Percentage of the 15-24 year-old population who are unemployed.
3. Data for Luxembourg are not included because the sample size is too small for a reliable estimate of the unemployment to population ratio.
Source: EUROSTAT (1997), *Youth in the European Union. From Education to Working Life*, European Communities, Luxembourg.

Chapter 4

Data for Figure 4.2 Expenditure on educational institutions for tertiary education, by source of funds, 1994

	Total expenditure from both public and private sources on educational institutions, as percentage of GDP	Private payments to educational institutions as a percentage of total expenditure (net of financial aid to students)[1,3]	Household payments to educational institutions as a percentage of total expenditure (net of financial aid to students)[2,3]
United States[4]	2.4	51.5	37.8
Australia[5,6]	1.8	25.3	11.9
Korea[7]	1.8	84.0	62.0**
Sweden[8]	1.6	6.9	n
Denmark	1.4	0.5	0.5
Turkey	1.3	5.9	5.9
France[4]	1.1	16.6	12.7
Hungary[9]	1.1	16.9	11.3
Japan[10]	1.1	53.5	50.8*
Mexico	1.1	18.9	18.9**
Austria	1.0	1.3	n
Spain[11,12]	1.0	21.9	16.3
United Kingdom [13,14]	0.9	n	n
Italy[15]	0.8	11.2	10.1
Greece[5]	0.7	n	n
Iceland[5]	0.7	7.1	7.1
Country mean	**1.2**	**20.2**	**15.6**

n: Negligible.
* Estimate by OECD Secretariat.
** Includes small volume of financial to students.
1. Payments for tuition fees and other fees, grants and contracts including those negotiated with employers for customised teaching, endowment income and alumni giving for tertiary education. Data refer to net private payments, i.e. after public financial aid to students and other subsidies to private entities attributable to private payment s to educational institutions are deducted.
2. Payments by students and their families for tuition fees and other fees for tertiary education. Data refer to net household payments, i.e. after public financial aid to students attributable to household payments to educational institutions is deducted.
3. Financial aid to students includes public grants, allowances and student loans attributable to private and household payments to educational institutions. It excludes amounts provided to students to cover living costs and other education-related expenses. It does not include tax breaks. For definitions and methodology, see OECD (1997), *Education at a Glance – OECD Indicators 1997*.
4. Excludes separately identifiable research.
5. Excludes private institutions.
6. Excludes vocational education and training institutions, open learning courses.
7. Excludes expenditure by regional-level authorities.
8. Includes all research.
9. Includes mainstream research.
10. Excludes allowances for children contingent on student status.
11. Partially includes research.
12. Partially includes private spending.
13. Includes public expenditure on research.
14. Excludes private household spending not subsidised.
15. Excludes private spending on vocational training in higher education.
Source: OECD Education Database.

Data for Figure 4.3
Growth in funding[1] for tertiary education by source in the early 1990s

Average annual percentage change

	Enrolment[2]	Public expenditure		Net household expenditure on educational institutions[4]
		Direct expenditure on educational institutions	Financial aid to students[3]	
Japan	3.1	5.6	5.5	5.2
Portugal	13.5	6.6	27.6	29.0
United States	0.8	1.4	11.6	5.4

1. Constant prices.
2. Based on headcounts.
3. Financial aid to students includes public grants, student allowances and the volume of student borrowing. The data do not include the implicit subsidy provided through tax breaks.
4. Net household expenditure on educational institutions refers to tuition fees and charges, less financial aid to students destined to institutions. Net spending by households is overestimated, because other forms of support (*e.g.* from employers or through tax breaks) or financial aid (student borrowing, particularly the implict subsidy components) for these expenditures are *not* deducted.
Source: OECD Secretariat, based on country-provided information for thematic review of the first years of tertiary education.

Japan: 1990-1995. Includes tertiary-level courses offered at special training colllleges and miscellaneous colleges. In these calculations, net household payments are given by gross tuition revenues. Financial aid is provided largely by the Japan Scholarship Foundation in the form of repayable loans at no or low interest, which are assumed to be applied toward education-related and living costs rather than tuition. Local authorities also provide financial aid for students, mostly in the form of loans. The subsidy component of student loans is, in any event, a relatively small share of the volume borrowed. Financial aid funded from private sources which reduces costs to students and their families has increased over this period, but remains modest. Ministry of Education, Science and Culture (1997), *Statistical Abstract of Education, Science and Culture*, 1997 edition, pp. 168-69; Japan Scholarship Foundation (1995), *An Outline of the Japan Scholarship Foundation*, Tables 2 and 3; country-provided information.

Portugal: 1990-1995. Includes private tertiary education. Direct public expenditure on institutions excludes specific funding for research. In these calculations, net household payments are given by estimated average fees in public institutions multiplied by the number of public tertiary education students plus estimated average tuition fees in private institutions multiplied by the number of private tertiary education students. For public institutions, the fees were Esc 1 200 in 1990 and 1995. For private institutions, average fees are assumed to have increased from Esc 300 000 to Esc 325 000 over this period. The number of students in public institutions paying fees is reduced by the number receiving grants; the latter are not obliged to pay fees. Grants for private tertiary education students, but not public tertiary education students, are assumed to be appplied toward tuition fees. New law calls for increases in fees for public tertiary education students and increases in funds for grants to all tertiary education students. Ministerio da Educação, Departmento do Ensino Superior (1997), *Higher Education in Portugal: A Report for the OECD*, Tables 6, 7 and 14; country-provided data.

United States: 1990-1994. In these calculations, net household payments are given by gross tuition revenues, less tuition remission and federal and state grants to students (including institution-financed shares of such grants). Student loans and other specially-directed financial aid are assumed to be applied toward education-related and living costs rather than tuition. Public expenditure on institutions is given by gross revenues from federal and state sources; financing for hospitals and auxillary activities are excluded. Public financial aid to students is given by the total volume of support available from federal and state programmes, excluding institution-financed shares of awards in such programmes. No account is taken of private third-party support to students not recorded in institutional records. U.S. Department of Education, National Center for Education Statistics (1997), *Digest of Education Statistics*, Tables 178, 324; The College Board (1996), *Trends in Student Aid: 1986 to 1996*, Tables 1 and 2.

Data for Figure 4.4
Household payments to educational institutions for education expenditure, participation rate and average duration of study, 1994

	Household payments to educational institutions as a percentage of GDP (net of financial aid to students)[1]	Participation rate (Age 17 to 34)	Average duration of studies[2] (in years)
Korea	1.10	12.4	3.4
United States	0.91	16.0	n.a.
Australia	0.22	14.4	n.a.
Mexico*	0.21	4.6	3.4
Spain	0.17	11.7	4.6
France	0.14	13.6	4.7
Hungary	0.13	n.a.	3.9
Turkey	0.08	5.6	n.a.
Italy	0.08	n.a.	4.2
Iceland	0.05	8.5	n.a.
Denmark	0.01	10.8	4.2
Austria	n	9.0	6.4
Greece	n	10.5	6.1
Sweden	n	9.2	n.a.
United Kingdom	n	9.3	3.4

n: Negligible.
n.a.: Data not available.
* Includes small volume of financial aid to students.
1. See notes to Data for Figure 4.2, p. 81.
2. For methodology, see OECD (1997), Education at a Glance – OECD Indicators 1997, Annex 3.
Source: OECD Education Database.

Data for Figure 4.5
Educational expenditure per student over the average duration of studies and final source of funds for tertiary education institutions, 1994

	Household payments to institutions (including financial aid to students) as a share of total expenditure on institutions[1]	Expenditure per student over the average duration of studies[2] (expressed as multiples of GDP per capita)
Hungary	11.3	3.16
Austria	1.3	2.75
Mexico	18.9	2.52
Netherlands	11.6	1.79
Denmark	0.5	1.76
Korea	62.0	1.50
France	12.7	1.46
United Kingdom	29.1	1.47
Greece	n	1.40
Spain	16.3	1.38
Italy	10.1	1.09

n: Negligible.
1. Payments by individual students and their families for tuition fees and other fees, and in this table include financial aid to students attributeable to household payments to educational institutions. Financial aid to students includes public grants, allowances and student loans; it does not include tax breaks. See also notes to Data for Figure 4.2, p. 81.
2. Cumulated as the product of unit costs and average duration of studies. For methodology, see OECD (1997), Education at a Glance – OECD Indicators 1997, Annex 3.
Source: OECD Education Database.

ALSO AVAILABLE

Redefining Tertiary Education (1998)
ISBN 92-64-16055-8
FF150

Human Capital Investment (1998)
ISBN 92-64-16067-1
FF150

Staying Ahead – In-service Training and Teacher Professional Development (1998)
ISBN 92-64-16076-0
FF135

Education at a Glance – OECD Indicators 1997
(Next issue forthcoming in November 1998)
ISBN 92-64-15622-4
FF260

Lifelong Learning for All (1996)
ISBN 92-64-14815-9
FF255

Prices charged at the OECD Bookshop.

The OECD CATALOGUE OF PUBLICATIONS and supplements will be sent free of charge on request addressed either to OECD Publications Service, or to the OECD Distributor in your country.

OECD PUBLICATIONS, 2, rue André-Pascal, 75775 PARIS CEDEX 16
PRINTED IN FRANCE
(96 98 05 1 P) ISBN 92-64-16128-7 – No. 50249 1998